Unlocking Your Superconscious Potential

Unlocking Your Superconscious Potential

The bridge between cutting-edge science and personal transformation

Anthony Leroy Williams

Founder of Mindset For Greatness Global Spiritual Center

Copyright © 2024 by Anthony L. Williams

First published in 2024 by Anthony L. Williams

All rights reserved. Published 2024. Printed in the United States of America. No part of this publication may be reproduced, stored in a retrieval system, transmitted in any form, or by any means—electronic or mechanical to include, photocopying, recording, or otherwise without written permission from the publisher.

The author of this book does not dispense medical advice or prescribe any treatment directly or indirectly, if you need medical, physical or psychological help please see a licensed physician. I am not a physician nor am I here to give psychological diagnostics or remedies. I am here to reveal a true path to personal transformation. If you use the information in this book the author and publisher assume no responsibility for your actions.

Unlocking Your Superconscious Potential

ISBN: 979-8-218-51456-3

Cover design: © 2024 Ajith Indike
Edited by Dr. Ann-Marie Y. Anthony-Williams
Interior design and typesetting by Anthony L. Williams

ISBN: 979-8-218-51456-3 (softcover)

Library of Congress Control Number: 2024924199

ALSO, BY ANTHONY L. WILLIAMS

INSPIRATION CORNER:

How to Induce the Right Inspiration that Transforms your Life from the Inside Out

*Available on Amazon

Unlocking Your Superconscious Potential

To my mother Daphne, thank you.

Acknowledgements

I am eternally grateful to the countless individuals who have contributed to the creation of this book. Their wisdom, support, and inspiration have been invaluable.

First and foremost, I want to express my deepest gratitude to my wife, Dr. Ann-Marie Y. Anthony-Williams, for her unwavering love, support, and invaluable editorial guidance. Dr. Anthony-Williams keen eye for detail and her unwavering belief in my work have been instrumental in bringing this book to life.

I am also indebted to my mentors and coaches, especially Christopher M. Duncan, whose wisdom and guidance have shaped my understanding of the human mind and spirit. Their teachings have inspired me to delve deeper into the realms of consciousness and personal transformation.

I would also like to acknowledge the countless spiritual teachers and philosophers whose insights have enriched my life and work. Their timeless wisdom continues to inspire and guide us all.

To my dear ancestors, who have paved the way for generations, I offer my heartfelt thanks. Their sacrifices and resilience have enabled me to reach this point in my journey.

Finally, I extend my heartfelt thanks to all those who have supported me on this journey, from family and friends to readers and colleagues. Your encouragement and belief in my work have been a constant source of motivation.

My utmost gratitude to the "All Indefinable Greatness," the source of all inspiration and creativity. It is through the grace of this higher power that this book has been brought into being.

CONTENTS

Introduction xiii
    The Bridge Between Cutting-edge Science and Personal Transformation xiii

Chapter 1 1
    Embracing the Power Within 1

Chapter 2 13
    Historical Echoes of the Superconscious 13

Chapter 3 25
    Unveiling the Hidden Architect of Our Reality ... 25

Chapter 4 35
    The Stalled Climber: Why We Get Stuck 35

Chapter 5 45
    The Integrity of Structures - Flowing Through Our Mental Landscape 45

Chapter 6 59
    Mindset Mastery - Becoming the Architect of Our Reality 59

Chapter 7 81
    Unlocking Our Superpower 81

Chapter 8 97
    Embodying Our Highest Potential 97

Chapter 9 113
    Way of the Superconscious Warrior 113

Chapter 10 129
    We Are the Creator: A Legacy of Light 129

Conclusion 153
    Your Journey Begins Now 153

References 157

Introduction

The Bridge Between Cutting-edge Science and Personal Transformation

In this book you will learn how to unlock your superconscious potential and be your own superhero.

For countless women, the glass ceiling looms as a formidable obstacle, an invisible barrier that hinders progress and limits potential. The relentless pursuit of career advancement can often feel like riding a pendulum, with each step forward met with setbacks. The aspirations seem shrouded in uncertainty. It is within this context of frustration and determination that a profound transformation awaits.

You will learn how to tap into your superconscious mind for guidance and move beyond what is keeping you stuck or oscillating. Breakthrough that infamous glass ceiling or just move forward to your goal. As well as structure your mind and life in such a way that leads you straight to your version of success.

You will learn how to use your superconscious mind to facilitate the quantum reordering process (QRP or recode) and remove all unconscious blocks. Learn how to use your superconscious for guidance. Learn how to get into the right mental structure that is needed to succeed. Learn a simple 6-step system that will help you manifest your intentions faster. Learn how to be it internally so you can project it physically (live it).

I stand before you, not as an infallible authority, but as a fellow traveler who has traversed the labyrinth of self-doubt and limitation. I have felt the scorching flames of adversity, the weight of unmet expectations pressing down upon me. Yet, from these ashes, I have risen, reborn with a newfound purpose. Like the phoenix, I have emerged from the flames, transformed and empowered. I share my story not as a boast, but as

Unlocking Your Superconscious Potential

an invitation to hope. For within each of us resides the potential for extraordinary transformation.

I have walked the path you are embarking on, and I know the challenges that lie ahead. I have sought guidance from mentors and coaches, and I have learned invaluable lessons along the way. Now, I extend my hand to you, offering the wisdom and compassion I have gained. Together, we can navigate the complexities of human experience, unlocking the hidden potential within. Let us embark on this journey together, hand in hand, as we create a future filled with limitless possibilities.

This book is your roadmap to unlocking the extraordinary potential within you. It's a fusion of ancient wisdom and modern science, designed to empower you to become the architect of your reality. I'm not peddling empty promises or quick fixes. This isn't about floating on a cloud of positive affirmations, hoping for miracles to fall from the sky. Instead, it's a grounded, practical approach that combines spiritual insights with tangible actions. I invite you to embark on a journey of self-discovery, where you'll learn to harness the power of your mind, body, and spirit. This is not about denying the challenges you face but about equipping you with the tools to overcome them. It's about mental alchemy, replacing fear with faith, doubt with determination, and limitation with limitless

Introduction

possibilities. Get ready to roll up your sleeves and do the work. Manifestation requires effort, dedication, and a willingness to step outside of your comfort zone. This book is for those who are ready to take control of their destiny. In it I share the exact 6-Step process I use. It's for the dreamers who are also doers, the visionaries who are grounded; remember, reality is relative. It's for individuals who are tired of settling and are ready to create a life of success and fulfillment. If you're seeking a magical formula or a guaranteed path to riches, this book may not be for you. However, if you're ready to invest in yourself and embark on a transformative journey, then you've come to the right place. Yet you may have what some believe to be magical moments. Welcome to the rest of your life.

In chapter one we will explore my story and how I ended up here as a transformational coach and author.

In chapter two we look into the rich history of the superconscious mind, tracing its exploration across ancient civilizations unto modern thought in the west.

In chapter three we unveil the hidden architect of our reality and take a deep dive into what is really driving our success and or failures.

In chapter four we look at the stalled climber: Why we get stuck, and the mentality program that is assigned to women and how it is holding them back. Here the concept of the placebo and nocebo are introduced.

In chapter five we consider the integrity of structures and why being in the right one is important for success. There is a structure for success and a structure that leads to failure.

In chapter six you are introduced to mindset mastery - becoming the architect of our reality. Here I put it all together giving you a sense of how to start the journey of mastering your life. "Change your mindset, change your future."

In chapter seven the simple process of unlocking our superpower is revealed; we look at different aspects of the mind and the role they play in producing and affecting our reality.

In chapter eight we embody our highest potential exploring how tapping into our superconscious mind can affect every area of our life in profound ways.

In chapter nine you are given the way of the superconscious warrior where we dive into what is required to live a superconscious life. We also look at and dispel some of the myths surrounding manifesting a life you love.

And chapter 10 reinforces that you are the creator, you are co-creating your reality and should leave a

Introduction

legacy of light for others to follow into greatness. I then leave you with some practical exercises.

So welcome, dear reader, to the extraordinary journey of unlocking your superconscious potential. In this book, "Unlocking Your Superconscious Potential," we are embarking on a transformative exploration of the untapped reservoir of power that resides within each of us.

At times, we may find ourselves feeling limited, held back by self-doubt, or trapped in the routines of daily life. But what if I told you that deep within you is a wellspring of extraordinary abilities, waiting to be rediscovered and harnessed? This is your superconscious, a realm of boundless creativity, intuition, and wisdom. As a matter of fact, there is the superconscious mind, the subconscious mind, the self-conscious mind, and the projected or outer mind.

Throughout this book, we will delve into the methods of accessing and embracing your superconscious mind. Still, we explore the total consciousness. I give you the techniques and practices that will empower you to tap into your innate potential, enabling you to navigate life's challenges with grace and confidence. Thus, enabling you to create the life you choose.

Unlocking Your Superconscious Potential

This book bridges the gap between cutting-edge science and practical self-development. I weave together the latest findings from **quantum physics, epigenetics, and neuroscience** to illuminate the incredible potential within you. These scientific disciplines are revealing remarkable truths about the mind-body connection, the power of intention, and the vast potential for personal transformation. We will also explore **ancient wisdom** that has guided human potential for millennia, finding fresh relevance in the light of modern science. Get ready to embark on a journey grounded in **evidence** and empowered by **practical tools** to unlock your superconscious mind.

By embracing the power within, you will unlock the doors to personal growth, self-discovery, and limitless possibilities. Together, we will embark on a journey of self-mastery, where you will learn to harness the power of your thoughts, emotions, and beliefs to manifest your deepest desires. You will then realize that all the books and courses you have invested in, thus far, on self-development were wrong. They all told you that there was something wrong with you. And that you must fix yourself in order to create. Not so at all!

Remember, dear reader, that you possess within you the ability to create the life you truly desire. It is a choice! The time to awaken your superconscious potential is now! Join me on this remarkable expedition

Introduction

to self-discovery as we unlock the door to a world of infinite possibilities.

Let me share a glimpse into my own odyssey, a tale of triumph over adversity. It is a story of shadows and light, of despair and hope. This is more than just a narrative; it is an invitation to embark on your own transformative journey. This is where it all started.

Let us embark on this transformative journey together and embrace the power within!

Chapter 1

Embracing the Power Within

A journey in search of the holy grail

Are you ready to unlock your superconscious potential?

Throughout the ages, great thinkers, philosophers, and spiritual leaders have recognized the immense power that is within our consciousness. From ancient wisdom traditions to modern scientific discoveries, the concept of the superconscious has fascinated and captivated the minds of those seeking to unlock the full potential of the human mind.

Now, it is your turn to tap into this source of power. As you embrace the power within, you will witness profound transformations in all areas of your life. Relationships will deepen and thrive as you tap into your intuition and connect with others on a deeper level. Your creativity will soar to new heights, as you access the well of inspiration that flows from your superconscious. And most importantly, you will experience a profound sense of purpose and fulfillment, as you align your life with your truest, most authentic life choices.

The Struggle

Lately, displacement and chaos seem to be a constant. That is, from viruses to lockdown, talk of war and economic crises, not to mention AI, robotics and the stock market crashing. But be very careful where you place your focus.

How are you supposed to reclaim your life when you feel like you have lost your mojo because you are lacking confidence or feeling not good enough? Is it possible to take back your life without spending years trying to *fix yourself?!* I bet you've tried all sorts of personal development that did not deliver as promised, yet, they were time consuming... And, nothing you tried has quite worked for you, right?

How do you find the TIME to do long workshops and meditations… if you're mentally drained, have a family or have a full-time job? Or all-the-above? How do you justify spending money on programs that don't work but are very time consuming if you barely have time to do it? Why's it so nerve-racking 'trying to change yourself' and position in life?

Is the constant battle to *fix yourself* to get your life back worth it? Can you really "take your life back" without trying to *fix yourself*? And when should you prioritize yourself? Should you even attend another workshop to try and *fix yourself*? Are you trying hypnosis and other modalities to make it work for you? How often? What about saying affirmations and positive thinking every day? *Who told you that you were broken in the first place?*

STOP. JUST STOP.

If any (or all) of the above is true or maybe this is your first attempt at changing your life… I can help you. The first thing I will tell you is that there is nothing wrong with you. So, stop trying to fix yourself! As one of my mentors, Christopher Duncan stated, it is "the personal development world [that] is broken!"

Taking My Life Back

Many of you reaching for this book might feel like you've hit rock bottom. Perhaps you, like me, once thrived in a demanding environment. You see, I was a successful marine. I guess one could say I grew up in the Marine Corps, so it became second nature to me. **Trading the uniform of a United States Marine** for civilian life, I felt adrift. Success in the Marines didn't translate seamlessly to the complexities of the civilian world. The transition was brutal. Financial security vanished, replaced by the harsh sting of barely making ends meet. **My confidence, once unwavering, crumbled.**

It wasn't just about me, I had to provide for my three children. As a single father, the weight of responsibility became an ever-present burden. **Child support became a sacred obligation,** and sometimes I would have to sacrifice a meal or two for myself so my son could have a great visit with me. Every other weekend, my son's presence filled the house with laughter, a beacon of hope amidst the struggle.

Then, life threw another curveball, yet it was one of love. **One of my teenage daughters came to live with me.** Suddenly, I was a single parent navigating the complexities of raising a teenage daughter. To top it all off, the first job I landed as a civilian vanished, leaving me feeling utterly defeated. Then there were two, my other daughter came to live with us for a short time.

This period was unquestionably my darkest hour. But within the ashes of despair, a spark ignited. It was a spark of **refusal**. I refused to accept this as my reality. **I refused to let my children inherit this struggle, and to let my then promised wife down.** This became the turning point, the catalyst that propelled me on a journey of self-discovery and ultimately, transformation.

My story isn't unique. Many of you reading this might share similar experiences. But here's the truth: **Rock bottom can be the most fertile ground for growth.** It's in these moments of profound challenge that we discover the strength and resilience we never knew we possessed.

This book is a testament to that strength. It's a roadmap I wish I had during those dark days.

I tried doing all sorts of different business, but nothing was working. As a matter of fact, my house was like a Christmas Tree, the lights were going on and off!

Because I could not pay my utility bills, yet most did not know my plight while I was living in that small blue shack.

My initial in-depth exploration into personal development felt like wading through a dense forest. An opening gift from my then-newly married wife, Ann-Marie, surprised me with an **Anthony Robbins course.** That ignited a stronger passion for delving deeper than my regular YouTube videos. There were countless paths, each promising a shortcut to success.

I dove into **EFT (Emotional Freedom Technique),** tapping away at my anxieties and negative patterns. **Hypnosis** offered a glimpse into the power of the subconscious mind. I delved into the world of energy healing by becoming certified in **Reiki** 1, 2, and master as well as exploring the principles of **Ho'oponopono.** I am certified as a practitioner and advanced practitioner. Dr. Michael Beckwith's teachings on **Life Visioning** also resonated deeply.

Each modality offered valuable insights, but a nagging feeling persisted – a sense of fragmentation. It was like assembling a beautiful mosaic, yet the pieces remained distinct, not forming a cohesive picture. This is where my story takes a dramatic turn. I manifested a remarkable mentor, Christopher Duncan, who introduced me to the concept of the **superconscious**

mind. This wasn't just another technique; it was a paradigm shift. The superconscious, Duncan explained, wasn't a distant entity, but rather our **innate wisdom**. It's the wellspring of intuition, creativity, and the blueprint for our highest potential. I became a certified coach in the **Magnetic Mind Method**, a system focused on being in the right structure.

Suddenly, the fragmented pieces of my personal development journey began to click into place. This realization became the key that unlocked a new level of transformation.

My Awakening

It was not until I manifested my last two mentors that I found the missing pieces: My last mentor, Duncan, passed the most crucial pieces to me. I had my first experience of the "superconscious Recode" from Duncan, opening my own untapped potential. Duncan then told me "I had to become it to see it!"

The superconscious work reviled my true self to me, by helping me confront my deepest limiting beliefs and challenged my previous understanding of personal development. I shed the need to "fix myself" and embraced the idea of co-creating with my superconscious mind. Thus, this work unlocked the power of my superconscious mind, allowing me to experience a shift in perspective while gaining new insights into my own potential.

I began applying my newfound knowledge as a Mental Alchemy Transformational Coach, helping others access their superconscious power and create lasting transformations. This work empowers them to become "Self-Conscious Creators" of their own lives.

So yes...not that long ago, I was in your shoes, or maybe worse off than you. Those early days were rough. I'd take a step forward only to take three more backwards. I was drowning in the feeling of not good enough. Anyways, if that's kind of how you feel right now, let me give you a life-compass. This way you can stop hitting dead ends or getting lost on back roads and instead, take the fast lane to regain and start living a life that you love. Make your sealing your floor!

Unveiling the Superconscious

Deep within you are a vast and potent power waiting– the superconscious mind. It's not a newly discovered concept. For millennia, spiritual traditions and ancient wisdom have alluded to this inner sanctuary. But now, science is catching up, providing a glimpse into the extraordinary capabilities of this innate intelligence.

The superconscious mind isn't simply another facet of your mind; it transcends the limitations of the self-conscious and subconscious. Think of it as our true essence, our **higher self**. Unlike the self-conscious mind, constantly bombarded by sensory inputs and fleeting thoughts, the superconscious operates from a place of profound stillness and infinite wisdom.

This inner wisdom is where our **intuition** resides – those gut feelings, sudden insights, or flashes of inspiration that often guide us in the right direction. It's also the source of our boundless **creativity**. Artists, inventors, and groundbreaking thinkers have long tapped into this realm, translating its whispers into groundbreaking ideas and artistic masterpieces. I also, as a poet, have tapped into its power to write amazing poetry.

At the time I was not aware of the source. As I recall, one night I needed to write an introduction to a spoken-word piece that I had written. I could not think of anything. I kept on drawing a blank as what I declared to be writers block. Tired and feeling defeated, I went to bed only to wake up at approximately 02:30 am with the whole introduction in my head. I wrote it down and went back to sleep. When I went to the studio the next day, everyone was amazed.

But the superconscious's power extends far beyond intuition and creativity. **Burt Hullinger's**

Unlocking Your Superconscious Potential

pioneering work – though perhaps not widely recognized by mainstream science – suggests a fascinating possibility. This possibility is the superconscious mind may hold the key to intergenerational inheritance of traits and abilities. Imagine accessing a reservoir of knowledge and potential accumulated over seven generations or more, passed down from your ancestors!

This is the true magic of the superconscious mind – it's the conductor of the symphony of our being. It **overrides** the limitations of the self-conscious and subconscious mind, filtering our thoughts and experiences through a lens of wisdom. It grants us the power to create the life we desire, but the key is in **knowing how to ask.**

By cultivating a connection with our superconscious, we unlock the doors to a life filled with boundless possibilities. We gain access to boundless creativity, solve problems with innovative solutions, and experience a deep sense of peace and purpose. This isn't just about achieving success, but about tapping into the very essence of who we are – a powerful, intuitive, and limitless being. Embrace the journey of exploration, and witness the magic unfold as your superconscious guides you towards a life beyond your wildest dreams.

Embracing the Power Within

Let me say, be prepared to be wowed as your life changes.

Unlocking Your Superconscious Potential

Chapter 2

Historical Echoes of the Superconscious

In search of the superconscious mind

The Superconscious in Ancient Egypt

The concept of a higher consciousness, often termed the superconscious, has intrigued philosophers and spiritual seekers for millennia. The Nile Valley, cradle of civilization, was also a crucible for profound spiritual exploration. Ancient Egyptians possessed an intricate understanding of consciousness, often symbolized by the human head surmounted by the divine falcon, a representation of the soul's ascent. The Book of Going Forth by Day, wrongfully referred to as the Book of the Dead, is a collection of funerary texts. These texts provides glimpses into Egyptian beliefs about the afterlife and the soul's journey. Still, Horus the Falcon head was and is a representation of higher consciousness.

Central to their cosmology was the concept of the Ba, often translated as "soul." This was not merely a disembodied entity but a conscious aspect of the individual that could travel between the physical and spiritual realms. The Ka, another essential component, was considered the life force, the vital energy animating the body. Together, the Ba and Ka, along with other soul components, represented different dimensions of consciousness.

While specific figures like the Greek oracles are often highlighted, Egypt's priestesses, or *heka*, deserve equal recognition. These **women** were revered for their wisdom and ability to access hidden knowledge. Their prophecies and divinations were seen as conduits for divine wisdom, suggesting a deep connection to a superconscious realm.

The Egyptian priesthood was particularly adept at inducing altered states of consciousness, often through ritual and meditation. These states were believed to facilitate communication with the gods and access to hidden knowledge. Oracle priests and priestesses, such as those at the Temple of Amun at Karnak, were renowned for their prophetic abilities. Their practices may have involved techniques that are similar to modern-day lucid dreaming or shamanic journeying, allowing them to tap into a realm of expanded consciousness. To this day the influence of this being Amun (the hidden one) pronounced Ah-mun stays with us. It is where the term Amen, Ah-men, Ay-men and Ameen or Ah-meen at the end of prayers came from.

The pharaohs themselves were considered intermediaries between the human and divine spheres. Their elaborate burial rituals and the construction of monumental devices like the pyramids indicate a belief in an afterlife and a continuation of consciousness. These structures, aligned with celestial bodies, may have been more than we originally thought; they could have served as energetic conduits or focal points for accessing higher states of consciousness.

While the specifics of their methods remain shrouded in mystery, the Egyptians undoubtedly possessed a sophisticated understanding of consciousness. Their exploration of the afterlife and the nature of the soul laid the groundwork for later philosophical and spiritual traditions. This exploration suggests a deep-rooted human fascination with the mysteries of the mind and its potential. Therefore, ancient Egypt offers a rich tapestry of evidence suggesting a sophisticated understanding of consciousness and its potential to transcend the physical realm. The ancient Egyptians, through their rituals, beliefs, and monumental architecture, appear to have tapped into dimensions of consciousness that continue to intrigue and inspire us today.

The Superconscious in Ancient India

Ancient Indian scriptures, such as the Upanishads, a philosophical text from ancient India, offer a profound exploration of consciousness. Central to their teachings is the concept of Brahman, often translated as the Absolute, or the Universal Consciousness. This is not merely a deity or a personal god, but an infinite, impersonal, and all-pervading reality underlying the entire cosmos.

Brahman is described as the ultimate ground of being, the source and sustenance of all existence. It is beyond attributes, yet the cause of all manifestation. The ultimate goal of spiritual seekers is to realize one's identity with Brahman. This realization, often termed as Atman or the individual soul, is identical to Brahman, a concept known as non-dualism or Advaita.

Historical Echoes of the Superconscious

To experience this unity, ancient Indian sages developed intricate practices, primarily meditation. Techniques like dhyana and pratyahara aimed to still the mind and turn it inward allowing the individual consciousness to expand and merge with the cosmic consciousness. The Upanishads offer a rich tapestry of metaphors and analogies to describe this journey, from the metaphor of the ocean and waves to the analogy of the clay and the pot. This profound exploration of consciousness laid the foundation for subsequent spiritual traditions in India, such as Buddhism and Jainism. It also influenced philosophical thought in other parts of the world, demonstrating the enduring power of these ancient ideas.

The Superconscious in the West

In the West, philosophers like Plato and Plotinus explored the idea of a transcendent realm beyond the physical world. They posited the existence of a higher reality where pure knowledge and eternal truths reside. These ancient thinkers intuited the presence of a superconscious mind, though they lacked the scientific language to fully articulate it.

More recently, figures like Carl Jung, a pioneering psychologist, introduced the concept of the collective unconscious, a profound departure from the individualistic focus of his contemporary, Sigmund Freud. Jung proposed that beneath the personal unconscious lies a deeper layer of shared human experience, a reservoir of archetypal images and symbols inherited from our ancestors.

This collective unconscious, Jung argued, is not a personal acquisition but a universal heritage. It explains the recurrence of similar myths, symbols, and archetypes across cultures and historical periods. The mother archetype, the wise old man, the hero's journey—these are not mere coincidences but reflections of the collective psyche.

Jung's work was groundbreaking in its recognition of a human interconnectedness that transcended individual psychology. While not explicitly using the term "superconscious," his concept of the collective unconscious points to a level of consciousness beyond the personal; a realm of shared human experience that resonates with the ancient idea of a universal mind.

Jung's theories have had a profound impact on psychology, philosophy, and spirituality which, inspire further exploration of the depths of the human psyche and our connection to something larger than ourselves.

Historical Echoes of the Superconscious

The Superconscious and Mystics

Throughout history, certain individuals have exhibited extraordinary abilities that suggest a direct connection to a realm beyond ordinary consciousness. Often labeled "prophets" or "seers," these individuals have reported accessing information and knowledge that seemed inaccessible through normal cognitive channels.

One of the most well-known figures is Edgar Cayce, the "Sleeping Prophet." In a trance-like state, Cayce could provide medical diagnoses, historical insights, and even future predictions. Cayce's ability to access information beyond his conscious awareness suggests tapping into a deeper level of consciousness that is, often referred to as the superconscious.

Other notable figures include Nostradamus, whose cryptic prophecies have fascinated generations, and the mediums of the 19th century spiritualist movement. While the validity of their claims is often debated, their existence points to a human potential for accessing information and knowledge beyond the ordinary.

These individuals serve as compelling examples of the human mind's capacity to transcend its usual limitations. Their stories challenge our understanding of consciousness and suggest that the boundaries between the physical and non-physical realms may be more permeable than we realize.

By examining the lives and experiences of these extraordinary individuals, we can gain valuable insights into the nature of the superconscious mind and its potential to be accessed and utilized by anyone.

These historical figures, from ancient sages to modern mystics, offer glimpses into the vast expanse of human consciousness. Their insights and experiences lay the groundwork for our exploration of the superconscious mind and its potential to transform our lives.

The Superconscious Mind Today

We've been conditioned to accept limitations, to believe that our potential is finite. But what if this isn't true? What if we are capable of far more than we can currently imagine?

The key to unlocking this extraordinary potential lies within our own mind. It's time to break free from the constraints of the ordinary and step into the extraordinary. We've been taught to follow the crowd and to play it safe. But true greatness comes from daring to be different from challenging the status quo.

Historical Echoes of the Superconscious

We possess an untapped reservoir of creativity, intuition, and wisdom. Our superconscious mind is a portal to a realm of infinite possibilities. It's time to awaken this sleeping giant within. By understanding and harnessing the power of our superconscious, we can rewrite our life story, overcome challenges, and achieve our wildest dreams.

Are you ready to embark on this transformative journey?

Unleashing Your Inner Potential

The journey to tapping into your superconscious mind begins with a shift in perspective. It's about recognizing that you are more than just a physical being; you are a spiritual entity with boundless potential. This isn't about denying the physical world but expanding your awareness beyond its limitations. Imagine your mind as an ocean. On the surface are the self-conscious thoughts, and just below is the subconscious mind of daily worries and the familiar patterns. But, beneath the waves remains a vast, unexplored depth—your superconscious. This is where intuition, creativity, and profound wisdom reside.

To access this deeper level, we must cultivate a state of stillness and receptivity. Meditation, mindfulness, and deep relaxation are essential tools. By quieting the mind, we create space for the superconscious to emerge. It's like tuning a radio to the right frequency; once you find the right channel, the signal becomes clear. Remember, this is a journey, not a destination. It requires patience, persistence, and a willingness to explore the unknown. With dedication and practice, we can unlock the extraordinary potential within us.

An Inspiring Story

Dr. Joe Dispenza's personal journey of overcoming a debilitating spinal injury serves as a powerful testament to the mind's extraordinary potential for healing. Diagnosed with a severe spinal injury that left him unable to walk, Dr. Dispenza turned to his own research and expertise in the mind-body connection for recovery.

Through a combination of meditation, visualization, and other mind-body techniques, Dr. Dispenza was able to rewire his brain and reprogram his body's response to the injury. Dr. Dispenza focused on creating a new reality where he was healed, visualizing himself walking, moving freely, and living a pain-free life.

Despite facing skepticism from medical professionals, Dr. Dispenza persisted in his approach, mentally putting his vertebras back together. Over a short time, he began to experience remarkable improvements. His pain subsided, his sensory function returned, and eventually, Dr. Dispenza was able to walk again.

Dr. Dispenza's story is a powerful reminder of the mind's incredible capacity to influence physical health. His experience demonstrates the transformative power of belief, intention, and the mind-body connection. It's a testament to the potential for healing when we harness the power of our minds. For the full story checkout "You Are the Placebo" (Dispenza, 2014, pp. xv-xxi).

SUMMARY

This chapter delves into the rich history of the superconscious mind, tracing its exploration across ancient civilizations and modern thought. We've examined evidence from ancient Egypt, India, and the West that highlight the enduring fascination with this concept.

From the Egyptian priestesses and the Vedic seers to the modern-day mystics, individuals throughout history have exhibited extraordinary abilities that suggest a connection to a higher consciousness. These figures, often labeled "prophets" or "seers," serve as compelling examples of the human potential to tap into the superconscious.

We've explored the concepts of the Ba and Ka in ancient Egypt, Brahman in Indian philosophy, and the collective unconscious in Jungian psychology. These ideas, while expressed in different languages and cultural contexts, converge on a shared understanding of a deeper level of consciousness.

By understanding the historical context of the superconscious, we gain a broader perspective on its significance. It's not a new-age invention but a timeless aspect of the human experience, recognized and explored by ancient sages and modern thinkers alike. This chapter lays the groundwork for our exploration of the superconscious mind in the present day, empowering us to unlock its potential for personal transformation.

Chapter 3

Unveiling the Hidden Architect of Our Reality

Understanding the landscape of consciousness

Limiting beliefs are like tiny cracks in a foundation. They may seem insignificant at first, but left unchecked, limiting beliefs can bring the whole structure crashing down. It's time to remove those cracks and build a foundation of empowering beliefs strong enough to support your wildest dreams

There are unseen forces putting up resistance and keeping you from your goals.

Our subconscious stores all our beliefs to include our negative and erroneous ones, and the body automatically responds in support of either. Have you ever felt a knot of anxiety tighten in your stomach before a big presentation, even though logically you know you're prepared? Or perhaps a wave of self-doubt washes over you despite years of experience? These are all whispers from your subconscious mind. This vast internal library houses every belief, experience, and emotion we've encountered, both positive and negative. Just like a well-meaning but outdated filing system, it can sometimes misfire, pulling up limiting beliefs or past anxieties that no longer serve us. The result? Our body reacts automatically, mirroring those outdated mental patterns. The good news is that by consciously reordering our brain, we can override our subconscious. Through practices like 21-days affirmations, first person visualizations, self-compassion, and the quantum reordering process (QRP) we can rewrite the narrative and empower our bodies to respond in a way that aligns with our highest potential.

We do not control our life self-consciously. Ninety-five percent of our lives is run by our subconscious mind for better or worse. Imagine your

Unveiling the Hidden Architect of Our Reality

mind as an iceberg. The self-conscious mind, the tip we readily see, represents only a small fraction – perhaps 5%. Below the surface lies the vast subconscious, estimated to make up a staggering 95% of the iceberg. This hidden realm stores our deeply ingrained beliefs, emotional patterns, and automatic responses. It's the musician in the orchestra, playing the familiar symphony of our lives – often without our self-conscious awareness. While this can lead to autopilot behaviors that serve us well, it can also perpetuate limiting beliefs and negative habits leading to failure. A major key to unlock true transformation is in acknowledging this power and learning to bridge the gap between the self-conscious and subconscious minds. By self-consciously directing our thoughts, feelings, and intentions, we can rewrite the script playing beneath the surface and create a life that aligns with our deepest desires.

Also, because this is our conditioned mind it was programed before we knew ourselves as us. Our subconscious mind operates on a fascinating timeline. Unlike the self-conscious mind that thrives on present awareness, the subconscious is a library of experiences and beliefs accumulated throughout our lives. Many of these programs were installed during our most formative years, even before we fully developed a sense of self. Like an old computer program running in the background, these subconscious patterns continue to influence our thoughts, feelings, and behaviors, without our conscious awareness. While these ingrained responses may have served a purpose in our childhood, they might not always align with who we are today. By taking the actions outlined in this book, we can make it an ally, not a limitation, on our journey to becoming our most authentic selves.

As a matter of fact, this conditioning created our personality. And our personality creates our personal reality. Imagine our lives as a magnificent tapestry, woven with experiences, emotions, and beliefs. The threads that form the very foundation of this tapestry are the result of subconscious conditioning – the imprints left by our environment, relationships, and early life experiences. These imprints, woven in before we even had a chance to consciously choose who we wanted to be, shaped our personality.

Now, here's the key. Our personality isn't a static entity; it's a dynamic program that constantly interacts with the world. Therefore, this creates our personal reality. If our conditioning led to a personality marked by fear, for example, we might subconsciously shy away from opportunities, attracting experiences that reinforce that fear. Yet, beauty is in the power of conscious awareness. By acknowledging these subconscious programs and their influence on our personality, we can begin to rewrite the script (Lipton,

2016, pp. 154-163). Through practices like meditation and self-reflection, we can choose new beliefs, cultivate new emotional patterns, and ultimately, weave a new personality. This, in turn, becomes the foundation for a new personal reality, one where fear is replaced by courage, and limitations give way to limitless possibilities. Remember, we don't have to be a product of our conditioning; we are the self-conscious architect of our reality, starting with the very threads of our personality.

Depending on how our subconscious is conditioned, our thoughts don't change, they become more prominent. As Dr. Donald Hebb's law states, neurons that fire together wire together creating a neuron superhighway. Imagine our subconscious as a vast neural network, a web of interconnected neurons shaped by our life experiences. Hebb's law is a cornerstone of neuroplasticity research, that beautifully illustrates how subconscious conditioning strengthens these neural pathways. When we repeatedly engage in a particular thought pattern, triggered by our early conditioning, those specific neurons fire together. This repetitive firing strengthens the connections between them, creating a "superhighway" for that thought pattern. The result? These conditioned thoughts become more prominent, readily accessible in our minds. They effortlessly influence our emotions, decisions, and ultimately, our reality. However, the good news is that the same principle applies to positive change. By consciously focusing on empowering thoughts, emotions, and beliefs, we can create new neural superhighways within our brains that ultimately alter our subconscious. Meditation, visualization, self-affirmation and right action are all tools that help us deliberately fire these new neural pathways, weakening the hold of our old conditioning. Remember, our subconscious is not a rigid prison; it's a dynamic landscape waiting to be reshaped. By consciously directing our thoughts and experiences, we can rewrite the script of our neural network and pave the way for a life that reflects our truest potential.

We are hardwired for success or failure. How this works is that our memories produce thoughts, and our thoughts produce emotions. These emotions activate a set of neurotransmitters in our brains which in turn creates a certain action as a response. However, after responding the same way over time, neuropeptides are created causing you to be addicted to that feeling and you create the same outcome over and over.

The Double-Edged Sword of Conditioning: From Habit to Addiction

Imagine your subconscious mind as a well-worn map, etched with the paths of our past experiences.

Unveiling the Hidden Architect of Our Reality

These experiences, particularly those from our formative years, create a network of memories that influence our present reality in profound ways. Duncan, in his work on neuro-linguistic programming, highlighted this beautifully in the magnetic mind method.

Here's the crux: these memories trigger thoughts, and as Dispenza emphasized, thoughts have a powerful downstream effect. Each thought ignites a cascade of emotions, activating specific neurotransmitters in our brain. These neurotransmitters, in turn, prompt a specific action or response. The problem arises when this cycle becomes repetitive.

Over time, as we respond the same way to similar situations, our brains start producing neuropeptides. These neuropeptides create a sense of familiarity, even pleasure, associated with that specific emotional response. Essentially, we become subtly addicted to the feeling generated by our habitual response. This "addiction" keeps us locked into a cycle, repeating the same outcome over and over, even if it's not necessarily a positive one (Dispenza, 2017, pp. 113-110).

The good news! Just as unconscious conditioning can create these "addictive" patterns, so self-conscious awareness can break free from them. By acknowledging the influence of our past experiences and the emotional responses they trigger, we can disrupt the cycle.

Unlocking Your Superconscious Potential

Through practices like meditation, mindful self-reflection and the QRP, we can choose new thought patterns, triggering different neurotransmitters. These different neurotransmitters, ultimately, create new and empowering responses. Remember, the map of our subconscious mind is not set in stone. We are cartographers, and with conscious effort, we can redraw the paths of our life, leading us towards success and fulfillment.

The conditioned mind may act like a foe at times, but it is here to protect us and everything it does is to this end. You see the conditioned/subconscious mind is the originator of the fight, flight, or freezing response (this is an action of the lower animal brain) and are unseen forces putting up resistance and keeping us from our goals. It knows what we have been doing year after year, because it is doing it. So, if we now decide we want to do something different, something that has not been experienced, it is deemed unsafe. Thus, our conditioned minds will keep this new goal at bay as this is seen as unsafe as it has not been lived. You see, if what we are trying to do has not been lived, it is unsafe for our conditioned minds that run the show. Therefore, we will not be, do, or have this new experience. This means that we are being kept in a state of reliving our past in different ways, but with the same results.

Unveiling the Hidden Architect of Our Reality

Simply put, the blueprint of our lives is based on the raw materials of our experiences. Unconsciously, our subconscious absorbs the habits, beliefs, and values of our environment, particularly during our formative years. These early imprints become the foundation upon which our personality is built. The people we surrounded ourselves with, the conversations overheard, the emotional climate of our home – all these elements contributed to the software that now runs our lives (Lipton, 2015, pp. 172-175).

. It's as if we were given a set of blueprints without our consent, and now we're navigating a world shaped by those original designs. But remember, blueprints can be revised. With awareness and intention, we can become the architect of our own destiny, redesigning our lives to reflect the masterpiece we envision.

The process of identification and transformation is a cornerstone of personal growth. Begin by observing your inner dialogue. What recurring thoughts hold you back? Challenge these beliefs with evidence to the contrary. Replace them with empowering statements that resonate with your desired reality. Remember, you are the author and predominant creative force of your life story. Rewrite the chapters that no longer serve you and watch as your world transform.

Unlocking Your Superconscious Potential

SUMMARY

This chapter delves into the hidden forces that can shape our lives without our conscious awareness. We've explored the concept of limiting beliefs, societal expectations, and the subconscious mind's role in creating our reality.

Limiting beliefs, often deeply ingrained, can create self-imposed barriers. Societal expectations, shaped by gender stereotypes and cultural norms, can subtly restrict our aspirations. These factors, when combined, can create a sense of stagnation and self-doubt.

The subconscious mind, a vast reservoir of memories and beliefs, operates below the surface, influencing our thoughts and behaviors. It's the origin of the fight, flight, or freeze response, often hindering our progress towards our goals. However, by understanding the subconscious mind's role and taking steps to reprogram it, we can break free from its limiting influence.

This chapter has empowered you with the knowledge and tools to challenge these invisible barriers. It's time to take action, to reclaim your power, and to step into the extraordinary woman you were always meant to be.

Chapter 4

The Stalled Climber: Why We Get Stuck

Exposing the invisible assassins

Her reflection in the elevator mirrored the beige monotony of her life. Ten floors, ten identical suits, ten years of climbing the corporate ladder, only to land on a rung that felt suspiciously like a dead end. Sarah squeezed her eyes shut, willing a spark, an escape hatch, anything to break free from the gilded cage of her own success.

There are Specific Obstacles in our Consciousness that can have us Stuck or Oscillating

You've undoubtedly heard of the placebo effect—the phenomenon where a person's experience benefits from a seemingly inert treatment, like a sugar pill. This fascinating concept has intrigued scientists and philosophers for centuries. Originating from the Latin word for "I will please," the placebo effect highlights the profound influence of the mind on the body. Historically, physicians recognized that even inert substances could induce healing responses, a testament to the power of belief. From the early use of sugar pills to modern clinical trials, the placebo effect continues to captivate researchers and underscores the intricate relationship between mind and matter.

But have you considered the flip side of this coin? Our world operates on a principle of polarity, every action has an equal and opposite reaction. Just as the placebo effect demonstrates the power of positive belief, there exists a counterpart, the nocebo effect. This phenomenon occurs when a negative expectation or belief leads to adverse effects, even in the absence of a harmful substance. Essentially, the nocebo effect harnesses the power of the mind to create negative outcomes. Undoubtedly, this expresses how our thoughts could materialize both healing and harm.

The Stalled Climber: Why We Get Stuck

Recognizing the potency of both the placebo and nocebo effects underscores the critical role of our mindsets in shaping our reality. By cultivating a positive belief system, we can harness the beneficial aspects of the placebo effect while minimizing the potential pitfalls of the nocebo effect.

Many women find themselves at a crossroads, feeling trapped by a sense of stagnation. At the heart of this feeling often is a complex interplay of factors. Limiting beliefs, treacherous and often unconscious, can erect formidable barriers to progress. The fear of failure, a universal human experience, can be amplified for women due to societal pressures to be perfect. Moreover, deeply ingrained societal expectations about gender roles and women's capabilities can create invisible chains that restrict ambition and potential. These factors, when intertwined, can contribute to a pervasive sense of being stuck, hindering personal and professional growth. To break free from these constraints, you must first identify and challenge these limiting beliefs, cultivate resilience in the face of fear, and redefine your own paths based on your unique aspirations rather than societal dictates.

The Illusion of Limitations

As stated, the human mind is a complex embroidery woven with threads of belief. For many of us, these threads are subtly tinged with limiting beliefs that cast long shadows over our potential. These self-imposed constraints, often rooted in subconscious programming, can manifest in various forms, from doubting our abilities to fearing failure. Remarkably, these beliefs can feel as concrete as physical reality, even when lacking substantial evidence. One's belief is so ingrained that if we attack it his or her body will have the same reactions as if we were attacking his or her life. That is powerful.

Despite the progress made by women in shattering glass ceilings and redefining success, the insidious nature of limiting beliefs persists. These invisible barriers, shaped by societal conditioning and personal experiences, can hinder women's advancement and create a sense of disillusionment. It's essential to recognize that these beliefs are not inherent truths but rather mental constructs that can be challenged and transformed. By illuminating these limiting beliefs, women can reclaim their power and step into their full potential.

The Silent Saboteurs: Societal Expectations

Beneath the surface of societal progress, a powerful undercurrent of unspoken expectations continues to shape women's lives. These invisible handcuffs, forged over centuries of gender roles and stereotypes, subtly restrict women's aspirations and achievements. From the pressure to prioritize family over career to the expectation of perpetual perfection, these societal constructs can create a sense of internal conflict and self-doubt. It's essential to recognize these invisible barriers and challenge them head-on. By dismantling these limiting expectations, women can liberate their true potential and forge their own paths to success and fulfillment. The power is in true choices, of what would you love to be, do, or have.

As a researcher and transformational coach, I've identified several deeply ingrained societal expectations that act as invisible chains, holding women back from reaching their full potential. Women today navigate a complex landscape shaped by unfair societal expectations that can be both subtle and insidious. The pervasive "Superwoman" myth, for instance, perpetuates the unrealistic expectation that women can effortlessly juggle demanding careers, perfect households, and fulfilling personal lives. While women are truly great at multitasking, there is a difference. This unattainable standard can lead to feelings of inadequacy, burnout, and a sense of falling short.

Moreover, the deceptive whisper of imposter syndrome can erode women's confidence, making them question their abilities and achievements. This internal critic, often fueled by societal messages about women's roles, can be a formidable obstacle to career advancement and personal fulfillment.

Finally, the "nice girl" trap, while seemingly innocuous, can stifle women's assertiveness and limit their ability to advocate for themselves. By conforming to the expectation of being agreeable and accommodating out of context, women may inadvertently undermine their own ambitions and well-being. For example, this can stifle women's assertiveness, making it harder to negotiate for promotions, express needs, or set boundaries – all crucial for professional advancement. Thus, these societal pressures, acting as invisible chains, can restrict women's potential and hold them back from reaching their full potential.

These societal expectations, deeply ingrained within the collective consciousness, create a powerful undertow that can pull women back just as they are on the verge of breaking through barriers. Like the undercurrents of a treacherous ocean, these unseen forces can be both insidious and overwhelming. Yet, within this challenge is an extraordinary opportunity. By recognizing these patterns, women can begin to dismantle the invisible assassins that bind them. Self-awareness is the first step towards liberation. Once identified, these limiting beliefs and societal pressures can be challenged and transformed. Through conscious effort and unwavering belief in one's potential, women can rewrite the narrative, creating a new story where ambition, power, and fulfillment coexist harmoniously.

Superconscious as Your Inner Compass

Amidst the complexities of navigating societal expectations and internal limitations, the superconscious mind emerges as a beacon of guidance. This higher level of consciousness, often untapped, offers an intuitive wisdom that transcends the limitations of self-conscious and subconscious. It acts as an internal compass, pointing towards our authentic path and empowering us to overcome obstacles. By cultivating a deep connection with our superconscious, we can access insights and solutions that lay dormant beyond the realm of logical thought. This inner wisdom can illuminate the path forward, helping us to break free from self-imposed limitations and align our actions with our deepest desires. As we learn to trust this inner voice, we discover a newfound ability to discern between what truly matters and the distractions that derail our progress. The superconscious mind empowers us to rewrite our story, to break free from the chains of societal expectations, and to step fully into our authentic power.

The Innkeeper and the Storm:

Imagine yourself on a treacherous mountain path, the wind whipping at your face and, rain stinging your eyes. You've been hiking for hours, drawn by the promise of a hidden paradise – a valley rumored to hold the key to true happiness. Your self-conscious mind, the enthusiastic traveler who, revels in the adventure. Yet, with every gust of wind and flash of lightning, a voice whispers from within, a voice that sounds suspiciously like your Aunt Mildred: "This is crazy! Turn back before you get hurt!" That's your subconscious mind, the ever-protective innkeeper, urging you to retreat to the familiar comfort of your routine. However, intuitive knowing calmly overshadows the subconscious mind with a clarity that navigates your path safely and directly to your destination. That is your superconscious mind, the wisdom bearer.

The Stalled Climber: Why We Get Stuck

SUMMARY

This chapter delves into the invisible forces that can hinder women's progress, exploring the concepts of the placebo and nocebo effects, limiting beliefs, societal expectations, and the superconscious mind.

We've examined how our thoughts and beliefs can shape our reality, influencing both positive and negative outcomes. The placebo and nocebo effects highlight the power of our mindsets to influence our physical and mental well-being.

Limiting beliefs, often deeply ingrained, can create self-imposed barriers. These beliefs, shaped by societal conditioning and personal experiences, can stifle ambition, foster self-doubt, and hinder progress.

Societal expectations, such as the "superwoman" myth and the "nice girl" trap, can further limit women's potential. These invisible chains can create a sense of internal conflict and hinder women's ability to assert themselves and pursue their goals.

Amidst these challenges, the superconscious mind emerges as a beacon of hope. This higher level of consciousness offers intuitive wisdom and guidance, empowering women to break free from self-imposed limitations and societal expectations. By tapping into their superconscious, women can reclaim their power, redefine their paths, and step into their full potential.

Unlocking Your Superconscious Potential

Chapter 5

The Integrity of Structures - Flowing Through Our Mental Landscape

Structure has integrity

Sometimes we may feel like puppets on strings; our lives dictated by forces beyond our control. From the invisible assassins to the unknown architects that shape our world that we didn't consciously design. This is the architect of structure – delivering a blueprint that either confines or liberates. In the following chapters, we'll delve into the intricacies of these structures by revealing how they can either imprison or empower us.

What is a structure? In its most fundamental form, a structure is a framework, a pattern that gives shape and stability to something. From the colossal expanse of a skyscraper to the intricate latticework within a single cell, structures are the building blocks of existence. But the realm of structure extends far beyond the outer physical world. The neurons in our brains are intricate structures, shaped by experiences, beliefs, and emotions. These mental architectures, often operating below the surface of consciousness, determine how we perceive, interpret, and interact with the world. From the grand structures of societal norms to the intimate architecture of our self-concept, these frameworks shape our lives in profound ways. Understanding the nature of these structures is another step towards engineering a life of purpose and fulfillment.

The Three Structures

A. Stuck Structure

The "stuck structure" is a rigid, inflexible mindset that hinders growth and progress. It's akin to being trapped in a mental prison, unable to see beyond the confines of one's current reality. This rigidity often stems from a lack of clarity about one's desires or an overwhelming pursuit of simultaneous multiple goals. Imagine trying to stretch a rubber band in four different directions at once; it loses its elasticity and snaps. Similarly, individuals attempting to juggle numerous aspirations without prioritization can find themselves paralyzed by indecision. Holding onto past hurts or clinging to dead-end situations further reinforces this state of stagnation. The consequences are far-reaching, manifesting as frustration, missed opportunities, and a general sense of dissatisfaction with life. Breaking free from this structure requires a willingness to embrace change, set clear priorities, and cultivate a growth-oriented mindset.

B. Oscillating Structure

The oscillating structure is characterized by a perpetual back-and-forth motion, a pendulum swinging between extremes. Consider the individual who relentlessly job-hops, driven by a simultaneous desire for independence and financial security, or the person who yearns for deep connection; yet, sabotages intimacy with emotional detachment. Chronic procrastination further exemplifies this pattern, as individuals oscillate between ambition and inaction, caught in a cycle of self-doubt and missed opportunities. This constant internal struggle not only depletes energy but also reinforces negative beliefs, creating a self-perpetuating cycle.

C. Flowing Structure

The "Flowing Structure" is flexible, adaptable, able to navigate challenges and opportunities; thus, allowing us to flow straight to our goals. This is the structure we want to be in. For decades, our understanding of biology was confined to the deterministic nature of DNA. However, the groundbreaking field of epigenetics has revolutionized this paradigm. We now know that our genes are not rigid blueprints, but dynamic expressions influenced by environmental factors, lifestyle choices, and even our thoughts. This paradigm shift empowers us to recognize that our biology is not merely a matter of fate, but a canvas upon which we can paint our own masterpiece. By understanding the intricate dance between our genes and our environment, we unlock the potential to optimize our health, well-being, and overall quality of life. Neuroplasticity tells us we can change the way we are hard wired.

Consider the graceful dance of a seasoned surfer. He or she rides the waves, not by resisting his or her power, but by harmonizing with his/her rhythm. This

The Integrity of Structures - Flowing Through Our Mental Landscape

adaptability is the hallmark of a life lived in flow. When faced with challenges or unexpected changes, those who thrive are not merely survivors but creators of opportunity. They adjust their strategies with fluidity, learning from mistakes as steppingstones to growth. Like the phoenix rising from the ashes, they embrace transformation, emerging stronger and wiser. This ability to navigate life's currents with grace and resilience is not innate but cultivated through conscious practice and a mindset that views challenges as catalysts for evolution. This dynamic approach to life fosters a sense of urgency and empowers individuals to shape their reality rather than being shaped by it.

When we operate from a place of flow, our lives become characterized by a sense of ease and purpose. Progress, rather than feeling like a relentless uphill battle, becomes a natural byproduct of our alignment with life's currents. Fulfillment emerges from the harmony between our inner world and external experiences. Moreover, the ability to navigate challenges with grace and adaptability fosters a profound sense of control, not in a domineering way, but in the understanding that we are active participants in shaping our reality. This internal locus of control is the cornerstone of a truly empowered life.

Bridging the Gaps

At the heart of every structure lies a dynamic interplay of forces, most notably tension and compression or as we would have it resolution. Imagine an elastic band stretched to its limit. The tension created within the band seeks resolution; it yearns to return to its original state, forward or backward. Similarly, structures, whether physical or conceptual, are held together by a delicate balance of these opposing forces. When this equilibrium is disrupted, the structure seeks to restore balance. This principle is fundamental to understanding the resilience and adaptability of systems, from the biological to societal. By recognizing the inherent tension within structures, we can harness its potential for growth and transformation. Just as a stretched elastic band can propel an object forward, controlled mental tension can propel us towards our goals.

Life is a series of transitions, each demanding a shift in our internal architecture. Yet, our tendency is often to become trapped in either a rigid, "stuck" structure or a chaotic, "oscillating" one. The problem-solving structure, while this may seem essential for overcoming challenges, can become a prison when it's the default mode. We become so fixated on fixing what we think is wrong with us that we lose sight of what could be right. This can lead to a sense of being stuck

The Integrity of Structures - Flowing Through Our Mental Landscape

in a loop, repeatedly applying the same solutions to problems without achieving lasting change. Conversely, the oscillating structure, marked by indecision and constant shifts, prevents us from gaining traction. It's like trying to build a house on shifting sands. To navigate these transitions successfully, we must cultivate a "flowing structure," a mindset that is adaptable, resilient, and focused on creation rather than mere problem-solving.

As hinted above, epigenetics may be The Hidden Code for Transformation. For decades, the blueprint of life – our DNA – was seen as an immutable code, dictating our traits and destiny. However, a revolutionary field called epigenetics has emerged, revealing a fascinating twist. That is, how our environment and experiences can influence how our genes are expressed, impacting our health, behavior, and even our future generations. What is Epigenetics? Imagine your DNA as a vast library containing all the instructions for building your body. Epigenetics doesn't change the actual code itself, but rather acts like a set of bookmarks and highlighters within this library. These epigenetic markers determine which genes are "turned on" (expressed) and which are "turned off" (silenced) in different cells at different times. This is known as the Transformational Power of Epigenetics. The exciting implication of epigenetics is that we have more control over our genetic destiny than previously thought. For more in-depth information on epigenetics please look up Lipton's work (Lipton, 2015, pp. 43-55).

Actionable Steps for Cultivating a Flowing Structure

To dismantle the structures that confine us, we must first illuminate their existence. Self-awareness is the cornerstone of this process. Journaling emerges as a potent tool for introspection, and remember we are only committing to paper what we want; not what we do not want. By committing thoughts and emotions to paper, we create a tangible record of our inner world. Through this process, patterns begin to emerge, revealing the underlying structures that shape our experiences.

Meditation, on the other hand, invites us to observe our thoughts and emotions without judgment. As we cultivate mindfulness, we gain a deeper understanding of the mental and emotional processes that drive our behaviors. This heightened self-awareness empowers us to identify the areas where we are stuck or oscillating, paving the way for conscious transformation.

Once we've illuminated our internal structures through practices like journaling and meditation, the

The Integrity of Structures - Flowing Through Our Mental Landscape

next step is to take action. Action involves a delicate balance of self-compassion and accountability. It's essential to recognize that self-awareness is not a destination but an ongoing journey like success. There will be moments of clarity and moments of confusion. The key is to approach these fluctuations with equanimity. By understanding that our internal world is dynamic and ever evolving, we can avoid the trap of self-criticism. Instead, focus on small, incremental changes. Celebrate our progress, no matter how small, and remember that transformation is a marathon, not a sprint. Yet, if we run full steam ahead into the unknown, I promise we will find our true self.

To transition from a fixed structure to a flowing one, we must cultivate a willingness to experiment and explore by stepping outside of our comfort zone and embrace novelty. Try new activities, engage in unfamiliar conversations, and explore different perspectives. This expansion of our experience horizon challenges the rigidity of our existing structures and opens doors to new possibilities.

It's not about abandoning our core values but about broadening our repertoire. By exploring diverse paths, we gain a deeper understanding of our strengths, weaknesses, and passions. This knowledge empowers us to make informed choices and design a life that truly resonates with our authentic selves.

Every experience, whether positive or negative, is a valuable data point in our journey of growth. Embrace challenges as opportunities for learning and adaptation. Instead of viewing setbacks as failures, see them as invitations to explore alternative approaches. Cultivate a curious mindset that welcomes new information and perspectives. By approaching life as a series of experiments, you'll discover hidden strengths and unlock unexpected potentials. It's not about perfection but about progress. Each step forward, no matter how small, brings us closer to a life lived in full flow.

Failure is an inevitable part of the human experience. Yet, it's how we interpret and respond to setbacks that truly defines our character and resilience. Instead of viewing failures as personal shortcomings, we must cultivate a mindset that sees them as valuable opportunities for growth. Each challenge is a chance to learn, adapt, and emerge stronger. By examining the circumstances surrounding a setback, we can identify underlying patterns or beliefs that may be hindering our progress. This self-reflection is crucial for unlocking new possibilities.

It's essential to detach from the emotional charge often associated with failure. Instead of dwelling on self-criticism, focus on extracting lessons (revelations) from the experience. What can you learn from this setback? How can you apply these insights to future endeavors? By approaching challenges with curiosity

The Integrity of Structures - Flowing Through Our Mental Landscape

and a growth-oriented mindset, we transform adversity into a catalyst for positive change. Every setback is a setup for a comeback.

Understanding

Consider the bank of a river, and the river flowing wherever the bank may take it through all the twists and turns. This is so because water follows the path of least resistance and therefore must stay within the structure of the riverbank. Just the same way energy follows the path of least resistance, and we as energy beings are no different. If we are going somewhere and there is a shorter route we will take the shortest route. How do we apply this to creating what we want? We must get into the right mental structure. You see most of us are in the problem-solving structure as stated above. We must learn to get into the creative structure by first looking at where we want to be; "Be it now" in the words of my mentor. This is where we put the power! Then, look at where we are now. By doing this, we enter the right mental structure to move toward our intended goal. Here we are using our higher energies against the lower vibrating energies. When done right, we create our path of least resistance that puts us in flow. Psychologically we create a sense of not being where we are supposed to be and must move toward the end goal. Just as in stretching a rubber band that seeks resolution, so to our minds will be seeking resolution towards our focus.

SUMMARY

This chapter explores three key concepts related to personal transformation: structures, epigenetics, and neuroplasticity.

Within the context of this chapter, structures are arrangements of elements that hold something in place. They can be physical like those holding up buildings, or mental, like those controlling our thoughts and behaviors.

The chapter discusses different types of structures, including oscillating (like a pendulum) and flowing (like a ship in motion).

Epigenetics studies how our environment and experiences influence gene expression. It's like having bookmarks and highlighters in our DNA library, turning genes on or off at different times. This offers exciting possibilities for transformation by optimizing health, enhancing brain function, and breaking free from limiting beliefs through lifestyle changes.

The Integrity of Structures - Flowing Through Our Mental Landscape

Neuroplasticity refers to the brain's ability to change and adapt throughout life. Our brains are not fixed structures, but constantly form new connections and prune unused ones. By consciously engaging in desired behaviors and challenging negative thoughts, we can literally rewire our brains for personality transformation.

The chapter emphasizes that these concepts offer powerful tools for personal growth. By understanding structures, epigenetics, and neuroplasticity, we can become active participants in shaping our own lives and unlocking our full potential.

Unlocking Your Superconscious Potential

Chapter 6

Mindset Mastery - Becoming the Architect of Our Reality

You must become the predominant creative force in your life to be the co-creator of your reality.

The All is Mind; the universe is mental, and we are a fractal of The All. The micro explains the macro and vice versa. We are to be co-creators. To introduce the concept of "Mindset Mastery" it is the ability to consciously shape our thoughts, beliefs, and attitudes to create the life we desire.

Misconception

Success is often misconstrued as a mere function of innate talent or talents or fortuitous circumstances. While these elements may play a role, they are far from definitive. The truth is, success is a complex interplay of factors, with perseverance, strategic thinking, structure and emotional intelligence often proving to be more potent predictors of achievement. It's a common fallacy to believe that those who reach the pinnacle of their fields did so effortlessly, solely due to their gifts. Countless hours of dedicated practice, coupled with a deep understanding of one's strengths and weaknesses, are the bedrock upon which lasting success is built.

Furthermore, external circumstances, while influential, do not have to dictate outcomes. Challenges are inevitable, but how we respond to them is what truly matters. Resilience, adaptability, and a growth mindset are essential for overcoming obstacles and seizing opportunities. Ultimately, success is not about perfection or luck; *it's about being the predominant creative force in your life* through, progress, learning, and the courage to keep moving forward, regardless of the circumstances.

The Battlefield of the Mind

We start out with a clean slate and develop memories via our subconscious and self-conscious mind which are referred to as two aspects of the mind. When we arrived here on earth, we were wide open to suggestions with our subconscious absorbing everything (i.e., the good, the bad and the ugly) in our external environment. Then, around age seven the self-conscious mind is on board. By this time, we are already preprogramed on what to think and our perceptions are tinted.

The superconscious mind has brought with it over seven generations of its own knowing. Yet, the superconscious does not care how we live; it will, therefore, give us what we ask for. Together, these aspects of the mind make up our memories. Our memories shape our thoughts, and our thoughts lead to our emotions which determine the reality we project into our lives. In context, this is what I call our projected mind- our reality. *One's Brain is likened to a holographic projector that shows his or her innermost beliefs on the screen of life.* Now based on our perception of objective reality that become subjective based on our filter aka programed mind. This causes an emotion that eventually leads to an action productive or destructive to what we want. With that being said, we all see things differently. The outcome reinforces the emotion that solidified a habit of good or bad. In essence we end up doing things in a way that is keeping our goals away from us and this is all unconscious to us. We start fighting to change, but as we fight the unwanted behavior becomes stronger. This is being in the problem-solving structure, but we need to be in the creative structure. For things to change we must change as our personality, literally, creates our personal reality. Over time we have developed certain limiting beliefs that show up as resistance when we try to create a new reality. There are six main resistances, which are listed below.

    Our minds and brains are exquisite instruments, capable of extraordinary feats of creation and comprehension. Yet, this same power can also become a prison, distorting our perception of reality. Like a lens through which we view the world, our thoughts shape our experiences. A pessimistic outlook can cast even the brightest day in shadow, whilst optimism can illuminate the smallest spark of hope. Our beliefs, fears, and desires combine to form a unique filter, selectively admitting information that aligns with our existing worldview while rejecting that which contradicts it. It is crucial to recognize the potency of our thoughts and to cultivate a mindset for greatness that empower us rather than limit us.

To truly live a life we love, we must learn to question our mental filters and challenge our assumptions. By doing so, we open ourselves to new possibilities and expand our capacity for growth and happiness. Just as a skilled photographer adjusts the lens to capture the perfect image, we can refine our mental focus to create a life that is rich, fulfilling, and aligned with our true potential.

Limiting beliefs - Negative Thought Patterns Holding us back from our full Potential

Limiting beliefs are the insidious architects of our perceived limitations. These are the negative thought patterns that, often unbeknownst to us, dictate the boundaries of what we believe is possible. They are the silent saboteurs of the unconscious mind whispering doubts in our ears, convincing us to settle for less than we choose. Rooted in past experiences and societal conditioning, such as fear of failure, these beliefs can be as restrictive as chains, binding us to a life far smaller than our true potential. It is imperative to identify and overwrite these mental constructs if we are to break free from self-imposed constraints and embrace a life of limitless possibilities.

To truly thrive, we must become conscious of the narratives we tell ourselves. Are we victims of circumstances, or are we empowered creators of our reality? Do we believe in abundance or scarcity? The answers to these questions reveal the underlying beliefs that shape our actions and outcomes. By shining a light on these limiting beliefs with a little shadow work, we can begin the process of exposing them and overwriting them with empowering beliefs. This can be done more efficiently via the quantum reordering process using the superconscious mind as you will learn later.

There are six major limiting beliefs that we usually work with that are common to almost everyone. They are:

1. "I'm not good enough,"
2. "I am not worthy"
3. "I don't belong"
4. "I am insignificant"
5. "I don't have the capacity"
6. "I am not perfect"

Negative self-talk is a pernicious habit that can erode our motivation, undermine our confidence, and cripple our decision-making. It's the relentless inner critic, a constant barrage of self-doubt and criticism that can leave us feeling overwhelmed and paralyzed. This insidious pattern of thought not only saps our energy but also distorts our perception of reality, leading to self-fulfilling prophecies. When we engage in negative self-talk, we focus on our perceived shortcomings rather than our strengths, hindering our ability to take risks and pursue our goals. Over time, this destructive cycle can create a downward spiral, making it increasingly difficult to break free from its grip. And to think, all this is happening in the background, unconsciously, unbeknown to us. You see our childhood memories became beliefs, which converted into thoughts that color our perception causing emotions that determine our actions, that give us a result that reinforces our thoughts and beliefs.

Reframing: Mental Alchemy of Transformation

Reframing is a powerful psychological tool that allows us to transform our lives by changing the way we interpret situations, experiences, and even ourselves. Reframing is becoming a mental alchemist, taking negative or challenging circumstances and turning them into opportunities for growth and empowerment. Here's how reframing can be used to create positive change:

Unlocking Your Superconscious Potential

1. Breaking Free from Limiting Beliefs:

As you know, our thoughts and beliefs shape our reality. Negative self-talk and limiting beliefs can hold us back from reaching our full potential. Reframing allows us to challenge these beliefs. Consider the thought, "I'm not good enough." By reframing it to "This challenge is an opportunity to learn and improve," we shift our focus from self-doubt to growth.

2. Increasing Resilience:

Life throws curveballs. Reframing helps us build resilience in the face of setbacks. Instead of viewing a failure as a personal defeat ("I'm a failure"), we can reframe it as a learning experience ("This didn't work out, but I learned valuable lessons for the next time"). This shift, in perspective, fosters a "growth mindset" and a willingness to keep trying.

3. Boosting Motivation and Confidence:

Negative interpretations can drain our motivation. Reframing helps us see the positive aspects of a situation. For example, a challenging task can be reframed as an opportunity to develop new skills and increase our confidence. This positive framing fuels our desire to 'take action' and persevere.

4. Building Positive Habits:

Reframing can help us create positive habits. Instead of viewing exercise as a chore ("I have to go to the gym"), we can reframe it as a way to invest in our health and well-being ("I'm taking care of my body"). This positive association increases the likelihood of sticking to a new habit.

5. Promoting Positive Self-Image:

Reframing can help us cultivate a more positive self-image. Instead of dwelling on our weaknesses, we can reframe them as opportunities for development. For example, "I'm shy" can be reframed as "I'm a good listener and observer." This shift in focus promotes self-compassion and fosters a sense of self-worth.

The Science Behind Reframing

Reframing isn't just wishful thinking (Harvard University, 2024). Studies show that reframing activates different areas of the brain, including those associated with positive emotions and goal setting. This brain activity can prime us for success and improve our ability to cope with challenges.

Reframing in Action and putting yourself into the right structure:

Here's an example of reframing in action:

Situation: You receive a rejection email for a job you really wanted.

Negative Reframing: "There goes that glass ceiling again. I'm not good enough. I'll never find a good job."

Positive Reframing: "This job wasn't the right fit, but it opens up the possibility for a better opportunity. This experience helped me refine my resume and interview skills." Make a true choice by seeing yourself being, doing and/or having it. If it is something you would *love* to be, do, or have. Then observe where you are now and act.

Mental Alchemy: Put yourself into the right Structure

Give me your hand and let me stand you upright. You could be my wife, mother, daughters, or sisters reading this book since I wrote it with women in mind and it will help all of you who follow through. Read this book at least seven times. You have been programed to think there is a glass ceiling and unconsciously you believe this to be true. This is in your subconscious mind and is not self-consciously thought of daily. It is a wrongful collectively accepted societal implant. Thus, unconsciously you are stopping yourself from grasping that desired position or you were made to believe only certain people make it in business. As a result, unconsciously you are incapable of reaching this level or even attempting to reach there. This is the unconsciously incapable phase.

But now I am telling you that anything is possible, and you are full of untapped potential. And the so-called glass ceiling is an illusion; its power is in you believing it collectively. You are to reframe this to know what you are going for is just self-challenging. Currently you know that all you must do is reframe that thought to create a new belief and accept the new emotions that follow. Accept the challenge; you now are self-consciously aware of being incapable of reaching your goal because of old programming. This is the self-consciously incapable phase. You are now aware!

However, just do the work by making a true choice (a true choice is something you want just to experience it, and there is no other reason; you just will love to experience it). Get into the right structure and become the predominant creative force in your life. For example, look at your intended reality and live it now. This is not like watching a movie, you must play the part, embody it. "You must be it now" as taught to me by one of my mentors who is a multimillionaire, and he learned this from a billionaire. After a few minutes, observe exactly how it is now. This will place you into the creative structure by creating a tension that must be resolved. Do this every morning and do everything possible that day toward creating that reality. You are now in the Self-consciously capable or competent stage.

Over time, as you continue to create new memories and emotions, it will solidify into your subconscious mind. This will become the image from where the reality of your life will be projected, as you build a new neuron superhighway to your intended reality. At this stage you are now unconsciously capable, and self-consciously see yourself in that role. This is the unconsciously competent level. By changing your personality, you change your personal reality. The body/subconscious can't tell the difference between what is actually lived and what is visualized. I think I have said that enough times now.

Reframing is a powerful tool that can be applied to any situation in life. By consciously shifting our perspectives, we can transform negative experiences into opportunities for growth, build resilience, and create a more fulfilling life. It's not about ignoring reality, but about finding a more empowering way to view it. Remember, you are the author of your story. Reframing empowers you to rewrite the narrative and create a life that thrives.

The Power of Visualization

Visualization is a potent tool for sculpting reality. It's the art of harnessing the mind's creative power to construct mental blueprints of desired outcomes. By engaging our senses and immersing ourselves in these imagined scenarios, we prime our subconscious for success. Our brains, unable to differentiate between vivid imagination and concrete experience, begin to align our thoughts, emotions, and behaviors with the envisioned reality. This mental rehearsal builds neural pathways that facilitate the manifestation of our goals. Thus, we can have it all now.

Think of visualization as a sculptor chiseling away at a block of marble. With each focused mental image, we remove what is not needed and those would be the obstacles and limitations that prevent us from achieving our full potential and reveal our true choice. This process not only boosts confidence but also enhances inspiration, as we begin to experience the emotional rewards associated with our goals before they are realized. By consistently practicing visualization, we cultivate a mindset of "being it now" and possibly, paving the way for extraordinary achievements.

How Visualization Work

The brain is a magnificent organ, capable of shaping reality through the power of thought. When we visualize our aspirations, we're essentially engaging in a neural construction project. Our brains, unable to discern between actual experiences and vividly imagined ones, begins to forge neural pathways that correspond to the visualized outcomes. These pathways, like well-trodden paths through a forest, become increasingly efficient with repeated use. As we consistently visualize success, our brains become primed for action, anticipating and preparing for the challenges and opportunities that lie ahead.

It's as if we're training our brains for peak performance. By mentally rehearsing desired outcomes, we enhance our ability to focus, make decisions, and respond effectively under pressure. This neural conditioning creates a fertile ground for manifestation, as our thoughts and actions align with our goals. The brain is incredibly malleable. With consistent visualization, we sculpt our own destiny.

Taking Action - Anchoring Our Mindset

The right structure is the fertile ground from which dreams take root, but it is through consistent action that they blossom into reality. While making a true choice, structuring and visualization are powerful tools, they are merely the seeds of potential. To cultivate a thriving garden of success, we must tend to those seeds with diligent care. This involves taking consistent, purposeful steps towards our goals, even when faced with challenges or setbacks. It's the dance between intention and execution that propels us forward, transforming aspirations into tangible achievements. **Success is not really a destination, but a journey marked by progress and perseverance.** The right mindset fuels our intensions, while consistent action propels us toward our objectives. By harmonizing these forces, we create a potent synergy that empowers us to overcome obstacles, learn from failures, and ultimately, to live a life aligned with our passions and purpose.

Anchoring is the art of creating powerful mental triggers that evoke specific emotional states. It's a technique derived from the principles of classical conditioning, where a neutral stimulus becomes associated with a particular response. By intentionally pairing positive affirmations or visualizations with specific anchoring such as a particular object, sound, or physical sensation—we can harness the brain's capacity for association to our advantage. These anchors become powerful tools that can be deployed in moments of doubt or challenge to instantly elevate our mood and mindset.

Imagine a lighthouse, steadfast and unwavering in its beacon. Anchors serve as our personal lighthouses, guiding us through the stormy seas of life. By consciously selecting and creating anchors, we equip ourselves with a potent arsenal for overcoming adversity and cultivating resilience. Whether it's a favorite piece of music, a cherished photograph, or a physical gesture, these anchors can become catalysts for transformation, propelling us forward on our journey towards fulfillment.

Anchoring is a versatile technique that can be tailored to individual preferences and needs. Affirmations, for instance, are powerful anchors that can be spoken aloud or silently repeated to reinforce positive beliefs. However, with affirmation part of you can be saying this is a lie. This is why using the "quantum reordering process" with the superconscious is the preferred choice. A simple yet effective affirmation might be, "I am capable, confident, and deserving of success" while emotionally remembering a time when you were. To make it effective, hold your wrist while the emotion of the memory is peaking and remove the hold before it peaks. You just created an anchor, and whenever you start feeling less confident, capable or deserving just grab your wrist. Practice and when you get it right the feeling will just come back and keep you on track. Mantras, shorter and more rhythmic, can be used to induce a state of focus and calm. A mantra like "peace and clarity" can be repeated silently or aloud to center the mind. Power poses, such as standing with hands on hips or in a victory pose, can physically anchor feelings of confidence and assertiveness.

Experimentation is key to discovering the anchoring techniques that resonate most deeply with you. Consider creating a personalized anchor ritual that combines multiple elements, such as a specific posture, a chosen affirmation, and a particular piece of music or smell. By consistently practicing these techniques, you'll strengthen the neural connections associated with positive emotions and beliefs, making them readily accessible in times of need. Remember, the goal is to create a toolkit of anchors that can be deployed at will, empowering you to navigate life's challenges with grace and resilience. I deploy many different anchoring techniques within my coaching program, Mental Alchemy.

One should stay focused on his or her goals and objectives regardless of any criticism or negativity from others. By maintaining a strong sense of self-belief and confidence in his or her work, one can prevent external factors from affecting one's emotional state. This can involve practicing mindfulness, setting boundaries, and prioritizing one's mental well-being to stay grounded and resilient in the face of outside influences. I challenge you to step up and take control of your life today.

Bonus Material

We are the directors of our destiny, the primary sculptors of our reality. Yet, for many, this inherent power remains untapped, obscured by layers of societal conditioning and unconscious patterns. We've been indoctrinated into a system that often prioritizes conformity over individuality, encouraging us to emulate prefabricated models of success. This external pressure can stifle our innate creativity and replace it with a desire to fit into a predetermined mold. It's time to reclaim our authorship and proclaim our authority, to step out of the shadows of expectation and into the spotlight of our own unique brilliance. Remember success is what we determine it to be for us; for some that may look like being a teacher and others a millionaire. No one can determine what success is for us but us. Do not fall into the societal conformity trap!

To truly thrive, we must become the protagonists of our own lives. This requires a conscious shift from

Mindset Mastery - Becoming the Architect of Our Reality

passive consumption to active creation. By understanding the forces that have shaped our beliefs and behaviors, we can begin to dismantle the structures that limit our potential. Hence the reason I have provided this information on your behalf. It's a journey of self-discovery, a quest to uncover our authentic desires and passions. Remember, you are not a product to be consumed but a force to be reckoned with. Embrace your individuality, trust your intuition, and dare to redefine success on your own terms.

As the predominant creative force of our reality, we must resist the allure of becoming passengers on the emotional pendulum. Emotions are a natural and essential part of the human experience. However, allowing emotions that are not self-consciously directed to dictate our actions can lead to erratic and unproductive behavior. When we surrender to the whims of our feelings, we relinquish control of our destiny, becoming mere spectators in the drama of our own lives. To achieve lasting fulfillment and success, we must learn to harness the power of our emotions, channeling them into constructive action rather than impulsive reactions.

To manifest a desired reality, we must cultivate a laser-like focus on our aspirations; therefore, resisting the temptation to dwell on past challenges or shortcomings. By anchoring our attention to the future we envision, we create a powerful energetic pull that draws us towards our goals. Conversely, fixating on the problems of the past traps us in a cycle of limitation, reinforcing the very circumstances we seek to transcend. It's essential to embrace our present reality, not as a point of stagnation but as a launchpad for creation. From this place of acceptance, we can consciously choose to design a new experience, driven by intention and imagination rather than a need for correction. You do not need fixing!

As such, we need to be it now, We should feel the same now as we will when we realize our new reality. We must be it to see it as taught to me by one of my mentors, or we will not see it and if we did it will be because we are oscillating back and forth to where we want to be and where we are. But never living the goal. Thus, before we attempt to create our new reality we must become the predominant creative force in our lives. We must learn to control our emotions knowing we are in charge.

Mindset Mastery - Becoming the Architect of Our Reality

SUMMARY

This chapter challenged us to take control and become the predominant creative force in our lives. Right now, our unconscious mind might be running the show, reacting to situations instead of consciously shaping them. Society often conditions us to follow pre-determined paths, but true transformation lies in taking the driver's seat.

Don't let your emotions control your journey. Reacting emotionally unconsciously creates an "oscillating" state, bouncing back and forth between your desired reality and your current one. Instead, find the right structure – a state of focus on your intended reality, not on fixing the old one. Remember, where your attention goes, your energy flows. Focus on the wrong thing, and you could be hindering your progress.

Learn to be comfortable with your present reality while actively creating a new one. Don't chase a new reality because you think it will change you – create it because you want to experience it. "Be it to see it" – embody the emotions and feelings associated with your desired reality as if it's already yours. This alignment between your emotions and your vision is crucial for manifesting your new reality.

We are shaped by our memories, thoughts, and emotions. These combine to form our projected mind, our personal reality. our perception of the world is filtered through our subconscious and self-conscious mind, which are pre-programmed from birth and our ancestral lineage. These filters can create limiting beliefs like "I'm not worthy" or "I'm not enough," acting as resistance to creating your desired reality.

Our brains, like the universe, operates holographically. Just as a hologram project an image from a reference point, our brains projects our reality based on our subconscious and self-conscious beliefs. To change our reality, we need to change the reference points - our ingrained beliefs and thought patterns.

Visualization is a powerful tool for creating a new reference point. By vividly imagining your desired reality, complete with the emotions, you'd feel as if it were true. You can rewire your brain and set the stage for manifesting your dreams. Imagine yourself already living your ideal life, "be it to see it". This is just the beginning. By taking control of your emotions, thoughts, and beliefs, you can become the architect of your reality and unlock the transformative power within you.

Chapter 7

Unlocking Our Superpower

Tapping into our higher selves unlocks our potential.

Have you ever felt a deep knowing, a certainty about something beyond the realm of logic? Perhaps a sudden wave of inspiration or a seemingly coincidental encounter that propelled you forward? This, my friends, is the whisper of your **superconscious mind**. In this chapter, we'll embark on a journey to unlock this incredible power and utilize it to **manifest your desires** with greater intention and ease.

The Symphony of the Mind

Imagine our mind as a magnificent orchestra.

The **self-conscious mind** is the listener and is supposed to choose the music it wants to dance to, making decisions based on logic and reason. This is also the aspect of mind that usually aspires to be wealthy, have better health, start a business, and live in a better home. This aspect of the mind seeks expansion. The macro dictates the micro as the universe itself is expanding.

The **subconscious mind** is the composer and houses our beliefs, habits, and memories; thus, playing familiar background music. The subconscious uses past experiences to determine what music we will dance to. The world we live in is subjected to polarity and all starts with the mind. This aspect of the mind wants everything to stay the same; it is there to protect us and prolong our life. Therefore, it likes to play familiar music which is anything that has been experienced. If a thing has not been experienced and survived it is deemed dangerous and unconsciously, the mind will do everything in its power to keep us from the unfamiliar.

The **superconscious mind**, however, is the virtuoso soloist capable of generating immense creative power with limitless possibilities and can change the familiar music. The superconscious is neutral and does not care if we live in a mansion or in a little blue shack; if we have a good paying job, making minimum wage; or if we are running a successful business. Therefore, once we tap into our superconscious mind, it will give us whatever we ask of it. The superconscious is our true creative self and our superpower. This superpower can supersede the other two aspects of mind and overwrite any resistance with new information. That is how we escape the familiar music. Think of it as the director of music or in Europe the conductor. We are learning how to tap into this field of information and unlock our potential.

The **projected mind** is the medium by which the agreed upon music is delivered as reality, just like a detailed hologram with loudspeaker drowning out everything else.

Awakening the Superconscious

Unlike the readily accessible self-conscious mind, the superconscious operates on a subtler level. Here are some ways to cultivate your connection:

- **Meditation:** Stilling the mind allows the superconscious to emerge from the background noise. Techniques like mindfulness meditation can create a clear channel for intuitive insights.

- **Nature Immersion:** Surrounding ourselves with the natural world fosters a sense of peace and facilitates a connection to something larger than ourselves. During meditation and visualization, we can immerse ourselves in nature walks.

- **Intuition Exercises:** Pay attention to gut feelings, sudden hunches, expansion in our heart and recurring dreams. These can be messages from the superconscious guiding us in the right direction.

- **Gratitude Practice:** Shifting our focus to appreciation opens us up to receiving abundance and aligns us with the frequency of the superconscious.

Superconscious Communication

The superconscious communicates in a unique language. Here's how to decipher its messages:

- **Synchronicity:** Pay attention to meaningful coincidences, repeating numbers, or encounters that seem divinely orchestrated. These can be breadcrumbs leading us on the path towards our desires.

- **Dreams:** Vivid dreams often hold symbolic messages from the superconscious. Utilize dream journaling and explore the symbolism to unlock hidden insights. Only we hold the key to any symbol we get.

- **Physical Sensations:** Tingling, goosebumps, or a sudden feeling of warmth or heart expansion can be signals of alignment with our desires. We must learn to trust our body's subtle cues.

Forming a Superconscious Partnership

- **Clarity of Desire:** We must be *crystal clear* about what we truly want to manifest. The stronger the intent, the more focused the message sent to the superconscious mind.

- **Belief and Trust:** Doubt acts as a barrier. Cultivating unwavering faith in our ability to achieve our desires and cultivating the power of the superconscious to guide us are essential. *Know that we are the predominant creative force in our lives.*

- **Aligned Action:** Action is the bridge between imagination and reality. Also *taking inspired action steps that feel aligned with our intuition and intended goal* is a must. Trust that the superconscious will orchestrate the details in ways we cannot yet imagine.

- **Innocence:** Learn to *cultivate a state of innocence*, for only in that childlike state will we be able to communicate with the superconscious mind. We must escape our senses and need to know, be in innocence (in no sense) and just be.

- **Communication:** Learn the different ways in which our higher-selves communicate with us individually. Study and experiment with muscle testing to find how yes and no answers are communicated through the body.

Living a Superconscious Life

By integrating these practices, we can become a master co-creator with the superconscious. We'll find ourselves:

- Making decisions with greater clarity and confidence
- Experiencing a deeper sense of purpose and fulfillment
- Attracting opportunities and resources that seem to magically appear
- Living a life aligned with our highest potential

**Remember, the superconscious is always working in the background.

Bonus Section: Overcoming Subconscious Resistance

While the superconscious is a powerful ally, it's important to acknowledge potential roadblocks. Here

Unlocking Our Superpower

are some common challenges and how to navigate them:

Fear of the Unknown: Stepping outside our comfort zone can trigger fear. If what we are venturing to accomplish has not been experienced or survived, it is deemed unsafe by the unconscious mind. We acknowledge the fear, but don't let it paralyze us. We trust that the superconscious is guiding us towards growth safely.

Limiting Beliefs: Deep-seated beliefs about our worthiness or capabilities can hinder progress. Practice affirmations, journaling, and self-compassion exercises to help create the mindset to rewrite these limiting narratives. You must journal every day and use the *quantum reordering process* (QRP) provided in this book.

Impatience: Manifestation takes time. Trust the process and focus on enjoying the journey. Celebrate small wins and stay committed to taking aligned action. There is a time allotted for every creation, from a chicken to a horse to a human being, the gestation time is different. We are embarking upon creating something new, thus, we must stay within the creative tension until its accomplishment. Keep in mind that it takes longer to grow an oak tree than a mushroom.

Advanced Technique: Accessing the Superconscious for Limitless Creation

For the truly dedicated, here's a powerful technique for superconscious creating: the wisdom process was taught to me by a multimillionaire. Here is my version of this powerful process, I call it "QRP".

One: Close your eyes, look into the quantum field of possibilities and choose your intended result/reality to be created. As you choose an outcome know that it already exists because the very act of choosing something means it exists. If it did not exist, you wouldn't have been able to think about it. Choose something you would just love to experience and for no other reason. Open your eyes and write it down, then cycle it.

Two: Enter a deeply relaxed state through meditation and/or breathwork. Closed eyes, place your hand on your chest and visualize your heart; take a slow deep breath and say I love my heart while seeing the breath encircling your heart and slowly breathe out. Use a rhythm that is comfortable for you. Do this six times while feeling a special love you have for someone. Remain present to the moment. This is how we create heart coherence. Heart coherence is taught by the HeartMath Institute.

Visualize your desired outcome in vivid detail, engaging all your senses (sight, sound, smell, touch, and taste). Evoke positive emotions associated with achieving your desire such as joy, excitement, and gratitude (*however you will feel once you have, be, or do it*). Remember, you must "be it to see it." Thus, you must realize that you have it now. Everything is created twice, first in the invisible (the mental and astral planes) and then the visible (physical plane).

Finish the structure by acknowledging the default creation that exists in your life right now. Note *how it is right now, exactly, do not sugarcoat it.* You just entered the structure of creative tension, and you must stay in it until your creation is birthed.

Three: Release the intention with trust, knowing the superconscious is working its magic. Maintain a state of innocence (in- no -sense) a state of not knowing and ask your superconscious what is the next step. Now pay attention to what you get, because if it is a symbol you may have to decipher it. Only you can do this by knowing what that symbol means to you, or you may just get a sense of knowing what is next. Just go with the flow! Sometimes you may have to just make it up and that is the first thing that enters your mind.

Unlocking Your Superconscious Potential

The Quantum Reordering Process

Once you have entered the creative structure and feel the tension of not being where you want to be, you will be drawn to your intended result. Remember tension seeks resolution and that means closing the gap toward your goal. Howbeit, as you move intentionally to your goal you may feel resistance. It could be a feeling of leaving your comfort zone, not being enough, or not being capable etc., as was mentioned before and is of unconscious origin.

The Superconscious Metaphor

Now imagine if you would that the vast ocean is the acting playing field of your life. You have been traveling in a sailboat on this ocean all your life in a particular channel and have deposited different memories, thoughts, and emotions that have manifested in your life. Yet, until now you did not realize that this is what has created your default reality; the reality that seems to repeat itself in different ways. Now, in your active playing field aka the ocean of these memories, thoughts and emotions are showing up as resistance that keeps you from going for your newly intended goals. It, also, keeps you going through the same channel of water.

Unlocking Our Superpower

In addition, these resistances show up as the waves, coral reefs and underling current that send you in the wrong direction by pulling you back. At the time of creation, they may have served a purpose, but now they are just obstacles in the way of what you are going for. So, as you travel along the channel or try to take a new one heading to your goal you are being stopped or pulled back by the underling current. What do you do? You call upon your superconscious mind letting it know your new choices and it will fulfil your wishes. The superconscious will pass over as a gentle breeze and stop the waves, remove the reefs and change the underling current to move in your favor. This will allow you to sail in a flowing manner to your destination. You do not need to self-consciously remember this metaphor or reread it. This metaphor is explicitly for the subconscious mind that remembers everything below the conscious level.

Connecting to your Superconscious

Four: With eyes still closed visualize being in your intended end results; what is your resistance level? On a scale of 0-10, 10 feeling like you are swimming upstream in mud with weighted shoes on. Zero you are swimming downstream with ease, how does it feel being, doing, or having what you want? Open your eyes and write down that number.

Five: Close your eyes and go into heart coherence as stated above falling into your heart field, feeling the love of a child you know or someone who loves you. See yourself as a little innocent child and step into that child. From the viewpoint of this child see a baby bird cracking through an egg in a nest, a representation of new life. Feel a sense of happiness and innocence falling deeper into your heart. Embrace your inner child and become playful and carefree. When you succeed in doing this you have found the holy grail, innocence.

Staying in this space ask your superconscious self, are you there? Then simply say I would like to communicate. Now pay attention to your body and note any changes in response to the question. For example, I usually get an expansion in my chest as a yes and a sort of butterfly feeling in my stomach as a no. Try it and keep doing it until you figure out how superconscious is communicating with you, because it is and always has been. You just have not been paying attention; that is about to change. Look up muscle testing, and become a part of our community for more information.

Removing Resistance

You will want to start out with something small like some kind of phobia as a test. Here, remember we

Unlocking Our Superpower

are always creating and never trying to fix ourselves. So, create the feeling of the opposite of whatever fear you have. For instance, we may want to create a life of confidence, assurance, love or even boldness. We can even be more specific, like having confidence while publicly speaking.

With your eyes still closed ask superconscious do you see the new reality I am creating? The old choices were created by default for a reason that is no longer valid. Please treat all resistance and all original events to include thoughts, beliefs, and emotions. Please overwrite all resistance to create an open flow toward my new choice. Trust your superconscious and take a few deep breaths. Now ask your superconscious to remove any residual resistance that's left over from this session. Notice how you feel.

Now open your eyes, take a 30 second break and visualize again being, doing, or having your intended reality/choice again and note the difference. On a scale of 0-10, what is your resistance level? You will find that it has moved. Some resistance may be bigger than others and need to be chipped away with a couple reordering processes. While others will be gone in one setting, the resistance will be moved.

Remember, the superconscious mind is a vast reservoir of wisdom and creative potential. By cultivating your connection and overcoming resistance, you can unlock a life of limitless possibilities, abundant miracles, and potential. The last and sixth step is to take aligned actions toward your goal every day. Be that person now.

SUMMARY

This chapter delves into the intricate workings of the mind, revealing the three primary players: self-conscious, subconscious, and superconscious minds. Each aspect plays a distinct role in shaping our reality.

The self-conscious mind, often associated with logic and reason, is the conscious aspect that seeks expansion and growth. It's the visionary, the dreamer, the part of us that sets goals and desires.

The subconscious mind, a vast reservoir of memories, beliefs, and habits, operates below the surface of consciousness. It's the guardian, protecting us from perceived threats and maintaining familiar patterns.

The superconscious mind, often untapped, is the virtuoso soloist capable of generating immense creative power. It's the source of intuition, inspiration, and limitless possibilities.

Unlocking Our Superpower

To navigate this symphony of the mind effectively, we must understand the interplay between these three aspects. The self-conscious mind sets the intention, the subconscious mind provides the foundation, and the superconscious mind orchestrates the manifestation.

By cultivating a connection with your superconscious, you can harness its power to overcome resistance, rewrite limiting beliefs, and create a life aligned with your highest vision. Remember, the symphony of your mind is in your hands. It's time to conduct the masterpiece of your own life.

Unlocking Your Superconscious Potential

Chapter 8

Embodying Our Highest Potential

Living a Superconscious Life by Embodying our Highest Potential

We've tapped into the extraordinary power of the superconscious mind. Now it's time to step into our role as a conscious co-creator. Imagine a life where every decision is a masterpiece, every relationship a symphony of souls, and every experience a catalyst for growth. This is the realm of superconscious living, where potential knows no bounds. Are you ready to embody your highest self and create a reality that is nothing short of extraordinary?

Unlocking Your Superconscious Potential

We've entered the realm of infinite potential within us. Now, let's dive deeper into how to integrate this awareness into the tapestry of our everyday lives. It's not just about fleeting moments of intuition; it's about cultivating a continuous connection that guides our choices, relationships, and experiences; ultimately creating lives we would love to experience.

Superconscious Decision Making

The superconscious is our inner GPS, guiding us towards our highest good. Yet, fear and doubt often overshadow its wisdom. To make superconscious decisions:

Trust your Intuition

Intuition, often dismissed as mere instinct, is a powerful compass guiding us towards our authentic path. It's the subtle whisper of the soul, offering insights beyond the realm of self-conscious thought. While logic provides a framework for understanding the world, intuition taps into a deeper wellspring of wisdom. When faced with a decision, trust the gentle nudge of your inner voice, even if it defies rational explanation. Your intuition is a trusted ally, offering invaluable guidance as you navigate the complexities of life.

Again, mindfulness is the art of cultivating present-moment awareness, a state of conscious attention to the unfolding of experience. By stilling the ceaseless chatter of the mind, we create a sacred space for intuition to emerge. Through other meditations, deep breathing, or simply observing our thoughts without judgment, we invite clarity and insight. As the mind quiets, we become more receptive to the subtle signals of our inner wisdom, allowing intuition to illuminate our path forward. Mindfulness is not just a technique; it is a lifestyle choice that empowers us to live with greater presence, purpose, and peace.

Embracing uncertainty is the cornerstone of personal growth and transformation. It is in the uncharted waters of the unknown that we discover our true potential. The subconscious mind craves certainty and predictability. It is precisely in the absence of these familiar anchors that we are forced to tap into our inner resources. By cultivating a spirit of adventure and curiosity, we invite the superconscious to guide us towards new horizons. Let go of the need to control every outcome and trust in the unfolding of life's mysterious plan. In the embrace of uncertainty, we find freedom, growth, and a deeper connection to our authentic selves.

While seeking guidance from experienced mentors and coaches can be invaluable, it is essential to remember that the ultimate authority on your life resides within you. External wisdom can offer valuable perspectives and strategies, but it is your inner compass that will lead you to your true north. Trust in your intuition and discernment to select the guidance that resonates with your soul. The most profound transformation occurs when we take ownership of our journey, relying on our inner wisdom to navigate the complexities of life.

Consider the following five CEOs who have publicly attributed their success to intuition or gut feelings, along with quotes that reflect their thoughts:

1. **Howard Schultz (Starbucks) **:
   - Schultz has often spoken about the importance of intuition in his decision-making process. Schultz once said, "Grow with discipline. Balance intuition with rigor. Innovate around the core. Don't embrace the status quo. Find new ways to see. Never expect a silver bullet. Get your hands dirty. Listen with empathy and overcommunicate with transparency. Tell your story, refusing to let others define you…" (Nisen, 2012).

2. **Anne Wilson Schaef (American Psychotherapist and Author) **:
   - Wilson Schaef emphasizes the role of intuition in

general by stating, "Trusting our intuition often saves us from disaster" (Schaef, n.d.).

3. ** Steve Jobs (Apple) **:
-Jobs believes we should have the fortitude to follow our intuition. Jobs warns, "Your time is limited, so don't waste it living someone else's life. Don't be trapped by dogma - which is living with the results of other people's thinking. Don't let the noise of others' opinions drown out your own inner voice. And most important, have the courage to follow your heart and intuition" (Jobs, n.d.).

4. **Jeff Bezos (Amazon) **:
- Bezos has been known to follow his intuition in business. Bezos said, "All of my best decisions in business and in life have been made with heart and intuition – not analysis. When you can make a decision with analysis, you should do so, but it turns out in life that your most important decisions are always made with instinct, intuition, taste, heart" (Hamilton, 2018).

5. ** Albert Einstein (Theoretical Physicist) **:
-Einstein has mentioned the importance of intuition in innovation and life. Einstein stated, "The intuitive

mind is a sacred gift, and the rational mind is a faithful servant. We have created a society that honors the servant and has forgotten the gift" (der Vliet, 2016).

These leaders exemplify how intuition can be a powerful tool in making decisions and driving success in their respective industries. Steve Jobs even went on to say that intellect was not as important as intuition because intuition had never let him down. I concur.

Superconscious Relationships

Relationships are mirrors reflecting our inner world. To cultivate harmonious connections:

We elevate our consciousness by cultivating a vibration of love, joy, and gratitude. Our energy is a powerful magnet, attracting experiences and people that align with our dominant frequency. By focusing on positive emotions, we create a resonant field that draws in abundance, harmony, and supportive relationships. Our thoughts and feelings are not merely internal states but energetic expressions that ripple outward, influencing our reality. Invest in raising your vibrational frequency and watch as your world transforms in accordance with your elevated perspective.

Authentic communication is the bridge between our inner world and the external reality. By speaking our truth with compassion and vulnerability, we foster genuine connections with others. When we communicate from the heart, we invite empathy, understanding, and reciprocity. It is essential to express our thoughts and feelings honestly, while also considering the impact of our words on others. Through authentic communication, we create a space for growth, healing, and deeper human connection.

Forgiveness is not about condoning harmful behavior but about liberating ourselves from the prison of resentment. By releasing the grip of past hurts, we create a spacious and open heart, inviting love, compassion, and inner peace. Forgiveness is a conscious choice, a powerful act of self-care that allows us to move forward with grace and resilience. It is through forgiveness that we heal our wounds, cultivate stronger relationships, and unlock our full potential for joy and fulfillment.

To deepen connection and cultivate shared meaning, consider creating sacred spaces within your relationships. Whether it's a dedicated room, a specific time of day, or simply a shared intention, these sacred spaces offer fertile ground for spiritual growth and emotional intimacy. Rituals, meditation, or shared affirmations can serve as powerful tools, grounding you in the present moment and fostering a sense of unity. These practices create a container for vulnerability, trust, and the free flow of energy between you. Remember, the most potent magic happens when hearts align and souls intertwine.

Superconscious Creativity

The superconscious mind is the wellspring of creativity. To tap into this flow and **unlock the full potential of our superconscious: We must quiet the incessant chatter of the inner critic.** By embracing experimentation and innocent playfulness, we create a fertile ground for creativity and intuition to flourish. This childlike state of wonder allows us to perceive the world with fresh eyes, unburdened by the weight of expectations and judgments. In this space of not knowing, we become receptive to subtle cues and synchronistic events that guide us towards our highest good. By surrendering to curiosity and embracing the unknown, we invite a profound sense of freedom and aliveness into our lives.

The most groundbreaking discoveries often arise from a place of playful inquiry. When we approach life with a spirit of experimentation, we open ourselves to infinite possibilities. Let go of the need to be right, to control outcomes, or to conform to societal expectations. Instead, embrace the joy of discovery and the thrill of the unknown. In this state of childlike wonder, we align ourselves with the creative force of the universe and unlock the extraordinary potential that resides within us all, our superconscious mind as our true self.

Collaboration can create a mastermind that transforms individual brilliance into collective genius. By sharing ideas, perspectives, and resources, we create a synergistic environment where innovation thrives. When we combine our unique strengths and knowledge, we unlock possibilities that would be unattainable alone. Through open dialogue, mutual respect, and a shared vision, we can build extraordinary things together. Collaboration is not merely a transactional exchange but a transformative journey that enriches both the individual and the collective spirit

Superconscious Health and Well-being

Our body is a temple for our soul. To optimize our physical and mental well-being:

The body is a complex and intelligent system that communicates with us through subtle signals. By paying close attention to hunger, fatigue, and pain, we gain invaluable insights into our overall well-being. Moreover, it's essential to recognize that physical ailments can often be rooted in unresolved emotional trauma (Babbel, 2010). These buried emotional wounds can manifest as physical symptoms, disrupting our sense of balance and vitality. By addressing the underlying emotional causes through techniques such as superconscious healing and energy healing, we can often alleviate physical discomfort. In some cases, these emotional imprints can be likened to dormant programs running in the background of our consciousness, occasionally interfering with our present-day functioning. By invoking the power of the superconscious to rewrite these outdated emotional scripts, we can dissolve their grip and restore harmony to the body and mind. I must note here that we are never trying to fix ourselves, but always creating; here the focus would be creating a life of health, fitness and vitality.

Self-care is not a luxury but a necessity for optimal well-being. Prioritizing sleep, nutrition, and movement provides the foundation for a healthy and balanced life. Adequate sleep rejuvenates the body and mind, allowing for optimal cognitive function and emotional regulation. Nourishing our bodies with wholesome foods fuels our energy levels and supports overall vitality. Engaging in regular physical activity reduces stress, improves mood, and enhances our connection with our bodies. By incorporating these essential self-care practices into our daily routines, we cultivate a strong and resilient foundation from which to pursue our goals and aspirations.

Nature is our greatest healer and teacher. Spending time in the natural world provides a profound opportunity to recharge our energy and reconnect with our inner selves. The earth's rhythms offer a soothing balm for our frenetic minds, while the beauty of the natural world inspires awe and wonder. Whether it's a solitary walk in the woods, a meditative moment by the ocean, or simply tending to a garden, immersing ourselves in nature allows us to ground our energy and find a deeper sense of peace and balance. Stand shoeless on the earth and allow the negative ions to flow through you into the ground.

Superconscious Living

Living a superconscious life involves contributing to the greater good.

Uncovering our life purpose is an invitation to embark on a profound journey of self-discovery. By aligning our passions with our core values, we create a powerful compass guiding us towards a life of meaning and fulfillment. Our unique combination of talents, experiences, and beliefs equips us with a distinctive contribution to offer the world. Embracing our true nature involves shedding societal expectations and embracing our authentic selves. When our actions are aligned with our purpose, we experience a sense of inner peace and a deep connection to something greater than ourselves.

Living a purpose-driven life is not about achieving a specific outcome but about embodying our essence. It's about waking up each day with a sense of excitement and anticipation for the opportunities that lie ahead. By aligning our careers, relationships, and personal growth with our core values, we create a life that is both fulfilling and impactful. Our purpose is an evolving journey, and it's perfectly acceptable to redefine it as we grow and change. Embrace the adventure of self-discovery and allow our unique light to shine brightly in the world.

Optimal health, vitality, and fitness are the birthright of every human being. When we align our bodies and minds with the natural laws of the universe, we tap into a state of vibrant well-being. This is not merely a physical pursuit but a holistic journey that encompasses nourishment, movement, and mental clarity. By prioritizing self-care and cultivating a deep connection to our bodies, we create a foundation for optimal performance, resilience, and joy. Our bodies are sacred temples, deserving of love, respect, and nurturing.

Embodying Our Highest Potential

Embracing a lifestyle of health and fitness is an investment in our future. It empowers us to live life to the fullest, experience greater energy, and connect more deeply with others. When we prioritize our well-being, we become an inspiration to those around us, fostering a ripple effect of positive change. Our bodies are capable of extraordinary things. By providing it with the nourishment, movement, and rest it needs, we unlock our full potential and live a life of vitality and abundance.

Living a life we love is the hallmark of a superconscious life. Life is a masterpiece to be created, not merely endured. We are not passive observers of existence but active architects of our reality. The most fulfilling lives are those lived intentionally, with a conscious choice to experience joy, passion, and abundance. This is not about selfish indulgence but about honoring our soul's deepest intentions. By daring to dream big and taking inspired action, we invite a life filled with wonder, purpose, and endless possibilities. Our happiness is not a destination to be reached but a journey to be savored along the way.

We choose to be the predominant creative force in our lives, not mere passengers on a journey but active co-creators of our reality. Each thought, emotion, and action contribute to the tapestry of our experience. By recognizing our innate power to shape our world, we step into a realm of infinite possibilities. We are not bound by the limitations of circumstance but empowered to transcend them through the forces of our imagination and intention. As co-creators, we partner with the universe, aligning our intentions with divine intelligence to manifest our dreams into tangible reality

Embodying the superconscious is a lifelong journey. It's about integrating awareness into every aspect of your life. Remember, we are co-creators of our reality. Trust your inner guidance, embrace challenges as opportunities for growth, and celebrate the beauty of being alive. The superconscious is our greatest ally in manifesting a life of purpose, joy, and fulfillment.

SUMMARY

This chapter emphasizes the importance of shifting from a passive observer of life to an active co-creator with the superconscious mind.

The superconscious mind is a guide and ally. It offers wisdom, intuition, and inspiration for navigating life's challenges and opportunities.

Embodying Our Highest Potential

Decision-making is enhanced by trusting intuition and embracing uncertainty.

Fear-based choices should be replaced with heart-centered decisions.

Relationships flourish when approached from a superconscious perspective. This involves open communication, empathy, and a focus on shared growth.

Creativity is ignited by tapping into the superconscious. Overcoming limiting beliefs and embracing experimentation are essential for unlocking creative potential.

Holistic well-being is achieved by nurturing the mind-body connection. Practices like meditation, mindfulness, and nature immersion support overall health and vitality.

Living a superconscious life involves service to others. Discovering one's life purpose and contributing to the greater good are essential components of fulfillment.

Ultimately, the chapter encourages readers to embark on a lifelong journey of self-discovery and spiritual growth, guided by the wisdom of the superconscious mind.

Unlocking Your Superconscious Potential

Chapter 9

Way of the Superconscious Warrior

Manifesting Our Superconscious Reality

Building upon the foundation of superconscious living, this chapter will delve deeper into the art and science of manifestation. We've explored the power of the superconscious mind and its role in shaping our reality. Now, it's time to harness this knowledge to create tangible results.

Understanding The Power of Belief

Our beliefs are based on memories that were formed at a very young age. These memories are not conscious to us; however, they are at the root of our project mind -aka-our reality. What we believe on a subconscious and self-conscious level ends up in our day-to-day living reality. Yes, as stated before, our beliefs create our reality. When we arrived here and entered our mother's womb, we were pure creative spirit coexisting with our mother, but something happened. Eventually we had to enter the world as an individual and experience life as a human being with all its challenges. When things did not go our way, we made up (and still do) the reason based on appearances that are sometimes illusionary. We also tried to justify the pain we felt, such as rejection, but that unconscious focus causes it to show up in our lives as not being good enough, or some other resistance that becomes a self-fulfilling prophecy. This makes it appear real or true for us since we are projecting it in our lives.

For example, between ages four to six we may have been in front of our class reciting something and the other children started laughing. In our little brains we coded up that they were laughing at us, when the fact is they could have been laughing at anything. However, because of this subconscious belief that we can't even recall, we are not allowed to do any public speaking. Our subconscious mind will not allow us to do it because it deems public speaking to be unsafe. I am using public speaking, but this could be on any subject or activity. Thus, many people are living their lives today from the point of view of a six-year-old. We should reevaluate everything we believe to be true and determine if it is aligned with what we are creating. If unconsciously and self-consciously we believe that wealthy people are bad, and we are trying to be wealthy it just won't happen for us. This is unless of course, you are or I am or intend to be a bad person. *Make a note here that it is the unconscious focus on the belief that gives it power; focus creates.*

Understanding the Law of Attraction

Let me tell you, the Law of Attraction isn't just a concept; it's a fundamental truth of the universe. It's the bedrock upon which your reality is built. You are constantly attracting things into your life, albeit they may not have been the things you wanted. Therefore, you are doing this unconsciously. Your thoughts are like magnets, drawing to you the very things you focus on. It's simple, yet profoundly powerful.

Unlocking Your Superconscious Potential

Think of our mind as a garden. What we plant grows. If we plant seeds of doubt, fear, or lack, expect a harvest of those same things. If we plant seeds of abundance, love, and prosperity, we can watch as our lives transforms into a bountiful garden.

Remember, we're not merely wishing or hoping. We're actively creating our reality. Our thoughts, feelings, and beliefs are the artists' brushes painting the masterpiece of our lives. So, choose wisely, my friend. Choose to be the predominant creative force in your life; choose to live your true nature and purpose. Choose to live a life of health, vitality and fitness. Choose to live a life you love for no other reason but to experience it. For in those choices are the keys to unlocking the limitless potential within us.

The trick is to change frequences and instead of creating from what is in the preprogrammed mind, we self-consciously invoke our superconscious potential. What is the law of attraction? The law of attraction is a secondary law, the law of vibration is what we are really working with, and the attraction factor is the effect. Energy attracts energy, and emotion or energy in motion sends out a vibration that attracts back to it the thing that is on that same vibrational frequency. Also, energy always seeks the path of least resistance. And right now, the path of least resistance is for most of us the whispers of the preprogrammed/subconscious mind. So, the path of least resistance is leading to our resistance that is keeping us from our goals.

However, we are changing this now by learning to connect with our superconscious mind and using the QRP. Still, we must learn to discern the difference between our superpower intuition and the whispers of the subconscious. Sometimes our deeply rooted feelings can masquerade as intuition. Thus, we must first realize that our thoughts and feelings are not real, because they are a result of perception, so turn off all familiar music. This is because our perceptions are tinted by unconscious memories from our distant past, and for some individuals suppressed trauma. We must *accept* what we don't want in our reality and then choose what we intend to create. Now go into innocence (in-no-sense) not knowing what is and then listen and realize there is a deeper knowing. This is not a knowing based on memory and emotions, but one of a higher origin that is received intuitively. This knowing can only be accessed in the present moment, the now where there is no past and no future, only now. This is where we find our superconscious self to really facilitate the law of attraction.

It's crucial to dispel common misconceptions surrounding the Law of Attraction. While it's a powerful tool, it's often misunderstood. Let's clarify some common myths:

Unlocking Your Superconscious Potential

- **Myth 1: Positive Thoughts Alone Manifest Reality:** While positive thinking is good, it's not necessary to manifest what we want, you read that right. *We only need to be in the right structure and not have any resistance to our intended outcome.* Structure has integrity! Consistent aligned action is equally crucial.

- **Myth 2: The Law of Attraction is a Quick Fix:** Manifesting our true choice may take time, patience, and persistence. All things have a conception, incubation, and birth period. For a woman giving birth it is about 42 weeks; for a chicken it's about two weeks; and for an elephant it's about 18-22 months. So, we stay in creative tension until the realization of our goals. That is, d*oing all we can every day towards our goals*. It's a journey, not a destination. This material being studied now, when put into practice, will speed up the learning curve and thus your process.

- **Myth 3: The Universe Will Provide Without Effort:** While the All-Indefinable Greatness to include the universe supports our desires, we must play an active role. We must *take aligned actions and make true choices*, this is essential. Take action today!

- **Myth 4: Focusing Only on the Positive Negates Challenges:** Acknowledging challenges is part of the process. Growth often emerges from overcoming obstacles. We must learn to *accept our current reality* and from there make a new choice. We use our current reality as a springboard to the new. Whatever we fight against must persist to be.

The Law of Attraction is a universal principle, not a magic wand. It's about harnessing your inner power to co-create your reality. *The magic wand you are looking for is you.*

Emotional alignment is a secret ingredient to manifesting your desires. Our emotions are powerful energy frequencies that attract corresponding experiences into our lives. When we cultivate vibrations of joy, abundance, and gratitude, we create a resonance frequency that draws these qualities into our reality. Conversely, emotions of fear, scarcity, jealousy or anger can create the very things we do not want and those would be our focus. It is the focus! By aligning our emotional state with our desired outcomes, we amplify the power of our intentions and accelerate the manifestation process. Our emotions are not just feelings but active vibrations we can consciously use to shape our world. It is important to remember that we will not get what we want, but we will always get who we are! This is why "we must be it now."

Overcoming Resistance

The superconscious mind is the alchemist's laboratory, where the raw materials of our intentions are transformed into tangible reality. We often encounter resistance on our journey towards our goals, a seemingly immovable obstacle blocking our paths. However, this resistance is an illusion, a fixed point in our subconscious mind that keeps us trapped in a cycle of frustration. To break free from this pendulum effect, we must elevate our consciousness by transmuting the fixed resistance into a volatile, malleable substance. When we operate from the superconscious level, we can reshape our reality with precision, replacing old, limiting beliefs with empowering new ones. This alchemical process is akin to quantum leaping, where we rewrite the underlying codes of our subconscious mind. This way, we create a new blueprint for our lives; hence, the name QRP.

It is essential to understand that willpower alone is insufficient for overcoming these deeply ingrained patterns. As a matter of fact, imagination will overcome willpower every time. Food for thought! While determination is admirable, it is the quiet power of the superconscious mind that enables us to bypass the limitations of the self-conscious and subconscious mind. By tapping into the infinite potential of our higher selves, we can dissolve the barriers that have held us captive, allowing our dreams to manifest with ease and grace. This is the true magic of creation—the ability to transform challenges into opportunities and limitations into limitless possibilities.

Shadow Work: Facing Our Darkside

Shadow work is the courageous exploration of the suppressed memories in the unconscious realm. It is the process of bringing to light the hidden aspects of ourselves that we have suppressed or blocked. Often, these shadow elements are rooted in fear, shame, or a desire to conform to societal expectations. However, feeling that is suppressed becomes repressed. By shining a light on these hidden corners of our psyche, we can begin the process of integration and healing. This involves acknowledging and accepting these darker parts of ourselves without judgment. We recognize that they are essential components of our human experiences. Through shadow work, we reclaim our personal power and create space for wholeness and authenticity.

Embarking on the journey of shadow work is not without its challenges. It requires courage, vulnerability, and a deep commitment to personal growth. However, the rewards are immeasurable. By integrating our shadow aspects, we develop a greater sense of self-compassion, resilience, and authenticity. We also free up immense amounts of energy that was previously consumed by hiding and denying these parts of ourselves. Start from a nonjudgemental space. Ultimately, shadow work is a transformative process that leads to a more conscious, empowered, and fulfilling life. The alternative is the repressed feelings being unconsciously expressed in the most negative ways.

It's about peering into the depths of our psyche to unearth the parts of ourselves we've consciously or unconsciously hidden and accept it. Journaling is a powerful tool for this exploration, allowing us to express our thoughts and emotions without judgment. Start by paying attention to your triggers and reactions. Observe what emotions arise unexpectedly. What patterns do you notice in your relationships? Answer yourself and work it out, but only actually write down what you want to manifest. Remember, shadow work is not about dwelling on negativity but about understanding your patterns and making conscious choices for growth. Meditation and mindfulness can also facilitate this process by helping us observe our minds without getting entangled in our thoughts. Dream analysis can provide profound insights into our subconscious, revealing hidden patterns and desires.

Shadow work is about watching and understanding these aspects of ourselves from a superconscious point of view. For instance, there is superconscious watching as a third party, and then your other aspects. It's about recognizing these hidden aspects as part of our human experiences and finding ways to integrate them into our lives in a healthy manner. This process can be challenging, but it's through facing our shadows that we truly step into our power and become whole. Just keep in mind, you do not need to know why or how long a particular resistance has been there or even what caused it to create.

The Role of Gratitude and Abundance

Gratitude is the cornerstone of abundance. When we focus our attention on what we already possess, we tap into a powerful energetic frequency that attracts more of the same. We all have some form of health, money, love, and happiness. Every aspiration and every intention already exist in the quantum field of possibilities, awaiting our acknowledgment. By expressing gratitude, we claim our birthright as co-creators of reality; and, we confirm that these intentions are already ours on some level. This is the essence of faith: Believing in what is yet to be physically seen. It's a paradox, perhaps, that we must appreciate what is before we can manifest what will be, but it's a fundamental truth. Consider the advancements of the past century: electricity, transportation, communication - luxuries unimaginable to our ancestors. Yet, here we stand, surrounded by these marvels. This perspective shift is essential. Gratitude is not merely a polite social construct; it's a conscious act of creation, a declaration of faith in the universe's abundance.

Taking Inspired Action

Aligned action is the bridge between intention and manifestation. It is the energetic counterpart to the visualization and intention-setting processes. While structure and visualization are essential, it is the consistent, inspired steps we take that transform aspirations into reality. Differentiating between forced effort and inspired action is crucial. Forced effort stems from a place of desperation or obligation, creating resistance and hindering progress. Inspired action, on the other hand, flows effortlessly from a deep connection to your purpose and passion. It feels aligned with your soul's purpose and brings a sense of joy and fulfillment.

To identify inspired action, we tune into our body's energy. When an idea or step resonates with us on a deep level, it often generates excitement and anticipation. We trust our superconscious intuition and follow the path of least resistance. It's essential to listen to our inner guidance and be open to unexpected opportunities. Inspired action is not about perfection but about progress. Celebrate small wins and learn from setbacks. By aligning our actions with our highest visions, we create a powerful momentum that propels us towards our goals.

Your Superconscious

Finally, our superconscious mind. It is the director of our orchestra-aka-mindset and can give us all that we want. Good or bad, negative or positive, it is here to experience life with no preference. The choices are to be self-consciously made by us. As we will have it, there is the director-aka superconscious. The composer/musicians-aka-subconscious and its preconditioned beliefs; and the music-aka-the project reality of the musician and the life we live. Then there is the listener and dancer to the music -aka-self-conscious mind. These make up the symphony of the mind. When we (self-consciously) try to change our reality the familiar music of the mind will continue to show up, causing resistance or oscillation and keeping us fixed in our reality. Every time we ask for different music to be played -aka-reality, - we will be delivered the same music. We can try talking with the composer/musician aka- subconscious but that will take time and is not always a success. However, when we go to the director-aka-superconscious, it can direct the musician to play new compositions of music. The musician is now playing with new beliefs. Thus, we can now realize the newly intended outcome with no resistance. Welcome to living superconsciously.

SUMMARY

This chapter delves into the profound impact of our beliefs on shaping our reality. We learn that our subconscious mind, influenced by early life experiences, often dictates our actions and outcomes without conscious awareness. These subconscious beliefs, whether positive or negative, act as a filter through which we perceive the world. To manifest our desires, we must first understand and transform these limiting beliefs.

The Law of Attraction is introduced as a fundamental principle governing the manifestation process. Our thoughts and emotions are likened to magnets, attracting experiences that align with our dominant vibrational frequency. However, it's essential to differentiate between mere wishing and conscious creation. Aligned action and emotional alignment are highlighted as crucial components of the manifestation process.

The chapter also explores the concept of shadow work, emphasizing the importance of acknowledging and integrating the darker aspects of ourselves. By addressing our shadow, we create space for personal growth and empowerment.

Gratitude emerges as a powerful tool for shifting our focus from lack to abundance. By appreciating what we already have, we open ourselves to receiving more.

The chapter concludes with an exploration of the superconscious mind, our innate connection to higher intelligence. By tapping into this level of consciousness, we can bypass the limitations of the subconscious and create lasting transformation.

Ultimately, this chapter empowers readers to become conscious creators of their reality by understanding the interplay between belief, thought, emotion, and action. It encourages readers to take responsibility for their experiences and to harness the power of their minds to manifest a life of abundance and fulfillment.

Chapter 10

We Are the Creator: A Legacy of Light

We are co-creators and the predominant creative force in our lives

This final chapter marks the culmination of our journey into the realm of the superconscious mind. We've explored the depths of our inner world, unlocked the power of manifestation, and laid the groundwork for a transformative life. Now, it's time to step into our role as a self-conscious creator and leave a legacy.

Unlocking Your Superconscious Potential

Let's take a moment to reflect on the profound insights we've uncovered. Let's revisit the core principles that have guided us thus far. That is, the nature of the superconscious mind—a realm of infinite potential that can be tapped into for profound transformation, the art of manifestation or alignment, the power of intention, and the significance of personal transformation. We've explored the intricate relationship between our memories, thoughts, beliefs, and reality by unveiling the power of our minds as a creative force. We've delved into the depths of our subconscious, uncovering limiting beliefs and harnessing the transformative potential of shadow work. This serves as a reminder of the incredible progress we've made. A cornerstone of our journey has been understanding the Law of Attraction and the role of gratitude in manifesting abundance. We've emphasized the importance of aligned action, differentiating between inspired steps and forced efforts. This has been a profound journey.

Remember, this is just the beginning of the journey. We've equipped ourselves with invaluable tools and insights. As we continue to explore and apply these principles, we'll unlock even greater levels of personal growth and fulfillment.

This knowledge is not mine; it has been here since time immemorial. I stand on the shoulders of giants.

We Are the Creator: A Legacy of Light

We invite you to step into a paradigm shift and to embrace the profound truth that we are not merely passive observers of life but active creators of our experience. We've been conditioned to believe that life happens *to us*, that we're passive recipients of circumstances beyond our control. This is a profound misconception. We are not mere passengers on this journey called life; we are the captains of our ships, the architect of our reality. Every thought, emotion, and action are brushstrokes on the canvas of our existence. Our beliefs are the foundation upon which our world is built. They are the blueprints from which our life emerges. Therefore, we must question our beliefs, challenge our assumptions, and replace limiting thoughts with empowering ones. This is the cornerstone of personal transformation. We hold the master blueprint within us, a divine architect shaping the contours of our reality. This is not a lofty concept reserved for a select few; it is our birthright. Overstand and internalize this truth, for it is the foundation upon which our journey of self-mastery is built.

Our thoughts are the building blocks of our world. They are not abstract entities but potent forces that shape our perceptions and experiences. What we believe becomes our reality. Cultivate a mindset for greatness, possibility, and limitless potential. Our beliefs are the lenses through which we view the world, and by refining these lenses, we can transform our perception of reality. We are not victims of circumstances but self-conscious creators of our experiences. Every choice we make is a declaration of our values and priorities. Are we living in alignment with our authentic self, or are we conforming to the expectations of others? Our actions are the physical manifestation of our inner world. When we live with intention, we're not simply going through the motions; we're creating a life of purpose and meaning. Each day presents countless opportunities to make conscious choices. We are to ask ourselves, "Does this action bring me closer to my desired reality?" "Am I honoring my values?" By aligning our actions with our intentions, we're laying the groundwork for a life of fulfillment and abundance.

Every choice we make is a brushstroke on the canvas of our lives. We are to live with intention, aligning our actions with our values and aspirations. Our purpose is not a distant destination but a guiding star illuminating our path. Embrace challenges as opportunities for growth, and apparent failures as steppingstones to success. By living with a sense of purpose, we infuse our lives with meaning; thus, creating a legacy that inspires others. We are not merely existing; we are expressing the divine potential within us. Our lives are masterpieces in progress, and we are artists. With each experience, we gain new colors and perspectives to add to our palettes. Embrace the beauty of imperfection, for it is in the imperfections that we find our greatest growth and resilience. We are not defined by our past mistakes or challenges. We are defined by our responses to them. Choose to learn, grow, and evolve. Our lives are canvases of infinite possibilities. We paint it with the vibrant colors of our dreams and aspirations.

Our journey of self-discovery and transformation is a beacon of hope for others and can be a catalyst for positive change in the world. As we evolve into our highest selves, consider the ripple effect of our wisdom. Our experiences, insights, and triumphs can inspire countless individuals to embark on their own journeys of growth. Our journeys are not merely a personal odyssey but are beacon of hope for those seeking their own transformation. So, share your personal story openly and authentically, allowing your light to illuminate the paths of others.

By mentoring, teaching, or writing about our experiences, we become a catalyst for change. Our words and actions can empower others to overcome challenges, unlock their potential, and live more fulfilling lives. The true measure of success is not solely personal achievement but the positive impact we make on the world. Our legacies are not defined by material possessions or accolades, but by the lives we touch. Be a source of inspiration, a guiding light, and a living example of the power of human potential. Our light has the capacity to ignite a flame in the hearts of others, creating a brighter future for all.

A Message from me to you

Personal growth is an eternal journey, a never-ending exploration of the human spirit. It is not a destination to be reached but a continuous process of expansion and refinement. Embrace the fluidity of life and let your spirit dance with the music of change. Stay curious, for within the unknown lies the potential for extraordinary growth. Commitment is the cornerstone of lasting transformation. Dedicate yourself to your evolution, nurturing your growth with consistent self-reflection and intentional action. Open-mindedness is the key to unlocking new perspectives and possibilities. Embrace the discomfort of the unfamiliar, for it is in these moments of vulnerability that true transformation occurs. Your superconscious mind is infinite in its wisdom and creativity. Continue to explore its depths, uncovering new dimensions of your being. Enjoy the journey, celebrate your milestones, and never stop seeking to become the best version of yourself.

Final Revelations

As you embark on this transformative journey, know that you are not alone. The universe we live in conspires in your favor, offering unwavering support and guidance. Trust in the inherent wisdom within you, for it is your most reliable compass. Your intuition is a sacred whisper, offering insights and direction. Listen attentively to its guidance, for it leads you towards fulfillment and authenticity.

Celebrate your victories, no matter how small. Each step forward is a testament to your courage and resilience. Embrace your successes with gratitude and joy, for they fuel your motivation and inspire further growth. Learn from your challenges, for they are the steppingstones to wisdom and strength. Every experience, whether positive or negative, contributes to your evolution. Embrace the revelations life offers and allow them to shape you into the person you are destined to become.

You are a divine expression of consciousness, capable of creating miracles. Believe in your limitless potential and allow your light to shine brightly. May your journey be filled with unwavering love, illuminating your path and warming the hearts of those around you. Embrace the infinite possibilities that await you and know that the universe supports your every endeavor. A powerful, intelligent force supports your every step, guiding you towards fulfillment and abundance. You are a divine being, a spark of the infinite consciousness of The All experiencing human form. Embrace this truth with unwavering faith. Your potential is boundless, your spirit is invincible. May your journey be filled with love, light, and the unwavering belief in your ability to create a life of extraordinary fulfillment.

Practical Exercises:

A well-structured morning ritual sets the tone for the entire day. It's a sacred space where you connect with your inner world and align your intentions. Begin by choosing activities that resonate with you. Meditation provides a tranquil start by quieting the mind to connect with your superconscious and fosters inner peace. Visualization allows you to envision your desired outcomes, programming your subconscious for success. Physical exercise invigorates the body and mind, boosting energy levels and clarity.

Grounding techniques, such as walking barefoot on the earth or spending time in nature, connect you to the planet's energy and promote stability. Journaling offers an outlet for self-expression, allowing you to process thoughts and emotions. Consider creating a dedicated journal for your morning reflections. Nature walks provide a serene environment for contemplation and inspiration, reconnecting you with the natural world and your superconscious.

Once you've established a grounding practice, it's time to set intentions for the day. What do you hope to accomplish? What qualities do you wish to embody? By clearly defining your goals, you create a focused direction for your energy. Making conscious choices throughout the day aligns your actions with your intentions. Reflect on your decisions by asking yourself if they contribute to your overall well-being and aspirations.

Creating an action plan provides structure and accountability. Break down larger goals into smaller manageable steps. Prioritize tasks based on importance and urgency. By taking consistent action, you move closer to manifesting your desires. Remember, flexibility is key. Allow your plan to evolve as needed and adapt to the ever-changing nature of life.

Consistency is the cornerstone of a successful morning ritual. Choose activities that you genuinely enjoy and can incorporate into your daily routine. Experiment with different combinations until you find what works best for you. Your morning ritual is a personal journey of self-discovery. Trust your intuition and allow the practice to evolve over time. By dedicating consistent time and attention to your morning ritual, you cultivate a powerful foundation for a fulfilling and purposeful life. Make your morning ritual a non-negotiable part of your day and watch as it transforms your life.

Connecting

Surrounding yourself with like-minded individuals is essential for personal growth and transformation. A supportive community provides a safe space to share your experiences, receive encouragement, and learn from others on a similar path. By connecting with people who share your values and aspirations, you create a powerful synergy that amplifies your potential. Whether you join an existing group or create your own, the collective energy of a supportive community can uplift and inspire you. This offers a sense of belonging and shared purpose.

The benefits of a community are immeasurable. Sharing your journey with others can help you gain new perspectives, overcome challenges, and celebrate successes. The support and encouragement of like-minded individuals can boost your confidence and motivation, propelling you forward on your path. Additionally, connecting with others who share your passions can lead to collaborations, partnerships, and lifelong friendships. By investing in your community, you not only receive support but also contribute to the collective well-being of others.

My Invitation

You are not alone on your path, and connecting with others who share your aspirations can significantly enhance your journey. I invite you to join our community of like-minded people that I have created just for this manual on Facebook. The name of the group is: "Unlocking Your Superconscious Potential" same as the book you are holding in your hands or reading on your device. There you can connect with me on a different level.

This final chapter is a celebration of your transformation and a call to action to share your light with the world. You have been initiated into the knowledge of the Superconscious Mind. You are the creator of your reality, and the possibilities are infinite. Celebrate the remarkable transformation you are undergoing. You have delved deep within, uncovering hidden strengths and expanding your consciousness. You have embraced your role as a creator, shaping your reality with intention and purpose. Now, it is time to share your light with the world. Your journey is a testament to the human spirit's resilience and the power of transformation. Inspire others to embark on their own paths of self-discovery, and together, we can create a world filled with love, compassion, and infinite possibilities. Thank you for reading this book. ☺

Note: All through this book I have used intentions or intended reality as what we are traveling toward. I have used desires sparsely because a wise man, a master of teachers, once taught me that "the fire of hell is the fire of desire in man." If you have a desire, it may never come to fruition, because it is something you just yearn for. I can crave food all day long and be really starving, and when I stay in that state it will be a living hell to me. But once I say after reading this book, I am going to get me something to eat, I just put out my intention. That is an intentional act created in my mind and once I take physical action this will resolve my hunger tension. This will change the state I am in. Tension seeks resolution and resolution is reached by following through with intention.

We Are the Creator: A Legacy of Light

SUMMARY

You've embarked on a profound journey, delving into the depths of your mind and unlocking the extraordinary potential within you. This book has unveiled the power of your superconscious, the art of manifestation, and the significance of personal transformation.

This is not just a book; it's a roadmap to a new reality. You are the creator, the architect of your destiny. The principles outlined in these pages are not mere theory but practical tools to shape your life.

As you step into this new chapter, celebrate your achievements. You've expanded your consciousness, challenged limiting beliefs, and awakened the sleeping giant within you. You've learned to navigate the symphony of your mind by aligning your thoughts, emotions, and actions with your intended result.

Now, it's time to share your light with the world. Your journey is a beacon of hope, inspiring others to embark on their own transformations. Become a mentor, a teacher, and a guide. Share your wisdom, your experiences, and your unwavering belief in the power of human potential.

Remember, you are not alone. There is a community of like-minded individuals who are also on this path. Connect with them, support each other, and create a ripple effect of positive change.

The possibilities are infinite. The future is yours to shape. Step into your greatness, embrace your divine nature, and let your light shine brightly.

Ancient Wisdom

Realization of the Seven Hermetic Principles

Alvin Toffler (1984) once said, "The illiterate of the 21st century will not be those who cannot read and write, but those who cannot learn, unlearn and relearn" (Forbes.com, 2022, p. n. d.). I think he was on to something here.

The Principle of Mentalism: The All-Indefinable Greatness

At the core of understanding our reality lies a fundamental principle: The All is Mind; the Universe is Mental. This suggests that the universe, in all its complexity and grandeur, is a mental construct. Everything that exists, from the smallest subatomic particle to the vast expanse of galaxies, emerges from a field of consciousness.

We are not separate from this cosmic mind but integral parts of it. Like ripples on a pond, we are manifestations of the underlying ocean of consciousness. This perspective challenges the notion of an external world separate from us. Instead, it proposes a unified field of existence where observer and observed are interconnected. I strongly believe to be true that this is one of the insights represented in the flower of life.

This concept, often described as panpsychism, suggests that consciousness is a fundamental property of the universe, not just a human attribute. Our minds, therefore, are co-creators of reality. Modern physics, particularly quantum mechanics, have begun to align with this ancient wisdom, suggesting that the observer influences the observed.

Armed with this understanding, we can begin to harness the power of our minds to shape our experiences. By consciously choosing our thoughts, we can influence the outcomes of our lives. It's a shift from being passive recipients of reality to active creators of it.

Ancient Wisdom

The Principle of Correspondence: Mirroring the Cosmos

The Hermetic principle, "As above, so below; as within, so without," encapsulates a profound truth about the nature of reality. It suggests a harmonious correspondence between the macrocosm (the universe) and the microcosm (the individual). We are, in essence, mirrors reflecting the cosmic order.

This principle implies that the laws and patterns governing the universe are mirrored within us. The same energy that orchestrates celestial bodies also flows through our veins. The same creative force that birthed galaxies is present in our thoughts and actions. This interconnectedness is not merely a philosophical concept but a tangible reality.

Dr. Thurman Fleet's (2000) assertion that physical ailments originate in the mind underscores this principle. Our bodies are physical manifestations of our mental and spiritual states. By understanding this correspondence, we gain the power to influence our physical well-being through conscious mental shifts.

The journey to mastery begins with recognizing the microcosm within the macrocosm. By attuning ourselves to the rhythms of the universe, we align with the natural flow of existence. This alignment is the foundation for personal growth, healing, and manifestation.

The Principle of Vibration: The Dance of Energy

Everything in existence, from the grandest celestial bodies to the smallest subatomic particles, is in a constant state of motion. This ceaseless vibration is the fundamental building block of reality. What we perceive as solid matter is merely a condensed form of energy vibrating at a specific frequency.

Consider the human body. At its core, it is a complex interplay of vibrating atoms and molecules, while an even deeper look will reveal that we are vibrating energy. Our thoughts, emotions, and intentions are also energetic expressions, each with its unique vibrational signature. This concept is beautifully sheathed in the adage, "As above, so below." The macrocosm of the universe and the microcosm of the human body are governed by the same principles.

Our feelings are particularly potent forms of vibrational energy. When we experience joy, love, or gratitude, we emit a high-frequency vibration that attracts similar energies into our lives. Conversely, negative emotions like fear, anger, or resentment create lower vibrational states that can manifest as challenges or obstacles. By consciously cultivating positive emotions, we can raise our vibrational frequency and align ourselves with the abundance and prosperity we desire.

Understanding the principle of vibration empowers us to become conscious creators of our reality. By mastering our thoughts and emotions, we can harmonize our vibrational frequency with our goals and aspirations; hence, accelerating the manifestation process.

The Law of Polarity: Duality and Balance

We live in a world of apparent opposite that is really the same. The universe operates on a principle of polarity, a dynamic interplay of opposites. Day and night, hot and cold, masculine and feminine—these are not separate entities but two sides of the same coin. This duality is essential for creation and growth.

Within our own consciousness, we experience this polarity as well. The self-conscious and subconscious minds, often in opposition, work together to create our reality. Like the poles of a magnet, they attract and repel, creating a dynamic tension. It's through the interplay of these polarities that we learn, grow, and evolve.

To master our reality, we must understand and navigate these polarities with wisdom. It's not about eliminating one pole in favor of the other but finding balance and harmony. Just as a pendulum swing from one extreme to the other, our experiences in life follow a similar pattern. The key is to find the center point, the equilibrium where both polarities coexist in harmony.

By understanding the law of polarity, we gain a deeper appreciation for the complexities of life. We recognize that challenges and setbacks are not necessarily negative but opportunities for growth. As we embrace the duality of our nature, we can recognize that both light and shadow contribute to our wholeness. We must always center ourselves.

The Principle of Rhythm: The Dance of Existence

Everything in the universe operates according to rhythm, a cyclical pattern of ebb and flow. From the cosmic dance of planets to the rise and fall of our breath, rhythm is the underlying pulse of life. This rhythmic nature is a direct consequence of vibration, the fundamental building block of reality.

Our experiences, too, follow a rhythmic pattern. Periods of joy and abundance are often followed by challenges and setbacks. This is not a cause for despair but an inherent aspect of the human experience. Just as night follows day, so too do periods of expansion and contraction.

However, we need not be passive victims of these cycles. By understanding the principle of rhythm, we can anticipate these fluctuations and prepare accordingly. Just as a skilled surfer rides the waves, we can learn to navigate the ups and downs of life with grace and resilience.

The key lies in maintaining a higher vibrational frequency. By cultivating positive thoughts, positive emotions, and actions, we can elevate our baseline and mitigate the impact of negative cycles. This isn't about denying the challenges but about approaching them with a sense of perspective and empowerment. Every ending is also a beginning, and within every challenge lies an opportunity for growth. Thus, hitting rock bottom could be your space for positive growth as desperation can be the catalyst for inspiration.

The Principle of Cause & Effect: Sowing and Reaping

Every action, thought, and emotion sets in motion a chain of events that ultimately shape our reality. This fundamental principle, often referred to as karma, suggests that nothing happens by chance. Our experiences are the harvest of seeds we've sown, consciously or unconsciously.

Our minds are the fertile ground from which our lives spring forth. The thoughts we cultivate become the blueprints for our reality. Negative thought patterns can lead to undesirable outcomes, while positive and constructive thinking paves the way for abundance and fulfillment. It's essential to recognize that even our subconscious beliefs, formed through early life experiences, continue to influence our present circumstances.

To harness the power of cause and effect, we must become conscious creators. By understanding the connection between our thoughts, feelings, and actions, we can begin to engineer the life we desire. This requires self-awareness, discipline, and a willingness to take responsibility for our experiences. Remember, every choice you make is a seed planted in the garden of your life. Cultivate it with care and reap a bountiful harvest. Also, both a poisonous tree and a life sustaining fruit tree will grow from the very same soil.

The Principal of Gender: Polarity in Creation

Ancient Wisdom

The principle of gender reflects the fundamental duality inherent in the universe. Just as the physical world is composed of masculine and feminine energies, so too is the realm of consciousness. The interplay of these polar forces is essential for creation, growth, and balance.

In the realm of physics, we observe this duality in the form of positive and negative charges, attraction and repulsion. In biology, it manifests as the male and female principles, necessary for procreation. Similarly, in the realm of consciousness, there is a dynamic interplay between active, assertive energy (often associated with masculine qualities) and receptive, nurturing energy (often associated with feminine qualities).

To manifest our desires, we must engage both aspects of our being. The self-conscious mind, often associated with masculine energy, initiates the creative process; while, the subconscious mind, with its receptive nature, incubates and brings forth the manifestation. This dance between intention and incubation is essential for realizing our goals.

It's important to note that gender is a spectrum, and these archetypes can be expressed in various ways. The key is to honor the balance and interplay of these energies within us. By understanding the principle of gender, we can harness its power to create a harmonious and fulfilling life.

Conclusion

Your Journey Begins Now

Begin shaping your own future, you are a superhero.

You've reached the end of this journey, a testament to your courage and commitment to personal growth. This book has unveiled the profound potential within you, the power to shape your reality through the self-conscious application of universal principles.

We've explored the nature of the superconscious mind, a realm of infinite possibilities, and the significance of aligning your thoughts, beliefs, and actions with your intentions. You've learned about the importance of emotional alignment, the art of shadow work, and the power of gratitude. We've delved into the fundamental principles governing the universe: Mentalism, Correspondence, Vibration, Polarity, Cause and Effect, and Gender. These principles, when understood and applied, can be transformative. Light bulb: You are subconsciously fighting your shadow self which becomes your unconscious focus. This is also true of your other resistances, when you should be integrating and rewriting to align with your superconscious self. Keep your focus in the higher vibration.

Remember, this knowledge is a tool, a compass to guide you on your path. It's up to you to wield it with intention and purpose. As you step into the world armed with these insights, trust your intuition, celebrate your successes, and learn from your challenges. You are a co-creator of reality and the possibilities are boundless.

Now, it's time to take action! Begin by incorporating the practices and principles outlined in this book into your daily life. As you embark on this new chapter called life, remember that you are the predominant creative force in your reality. Your journey is a continuous evolution, marked by growth, challenges, and triumphs. Stay curious, open-minded, and committed to your personal development. Practice self-care, and trust in the guidance of your intuition.

Conclusion

Create a morning ritual and explore the depths of your superconscious mind. Trust in the journey; for, it is in the unfolding of your experience that true transformation occurs.

Embrace your power, live with intention, and create a life that is a testament to your extraordinary potential. The world is waiting for your unique contribution. Share your light, inspire others, and become a catalyst for positive change. The future is yours to shape.

Congratulations on completing this book. Your journey of self-discovery has just begun.

References

Babbel, S., MFT, PhD (2010, April 8). *The Connections Between Emotional Stress, Trauma and Physical Pain*. Psychology Today. Retrieved October 20, 2024, from https://www.psychologytoday.com/us/blog/somatic-psychology/201004/the-connections-between-emotional-stress-trauma-and-physical-pain

der Vliet, T. V. (2016, October 26). Why the Rational Mind is Only There to Serve our Intuition. HUFFPOST. Retrieved October 19, 2024, from https://www.huffingtonpost.co.uk/tim-van-der-vliet/rational-mind-intuition_b_8388906.html

Dispenza, J., Dr. (2014). *You Are the Placebo: Making your mind matter.* (pp. xv-xxi). Hay House, Inc.

Dispenza, J., Dr. (2017). *Becoming Supernatural: How common people are doing the uncommon.* Hay House, Inc.

Fleet, T. (2000). Rays of the Dawn: Natural Laws of the Body, Mind, And Soul. Concept-Therapy Institute. ISBN 0-9671845-0-9 T. (2000).

Hamilton, I. A. (2018, September 14). *Jeff Bezos says all his best decisions involved intuition and gut, not analysis.* Business Insider. Retrieved October 19, 2024, from https://www.businessinsider.com/how-jeff-bezos-makes-decisions-2018-9?utm_source=copy-link&utm_medium=referral&utm_content=topbar&utm_term=desktop

Harvard University (2024). *Stress & Development Lab: Positive Reframing and Examining the Evidence.* Harvard University. Retrieved October 13, 2024, from https://sdlab.fas.harvard.edu/cognitive-reappraisal/positive-reframing-and-examining-evidence

Jobs, S. (n.d.). *Steve Jobs Quotes.* Goodreads. Retrieved October 19, 2024, from https://www.goodreads.com/quotes/374630-your-time-is-limited-so-don-t-waste-it-living-someone

Lipton, B. H., Ph. D. (2016). *The Biology of Belief: Unleashing the power of consciousness, matter &*

References

miracles. (pp. 43-55 & 154-163). Hay House., Inc.

Nisen, M. (2012). *17 Quotes from Starbucks CEO Howard Schultz on How He Became Successful.* Business Insider. Retrieved October 19, 2024, from https://www.businessinsider.com/howard-schultz-quotes-2012-11

Quote Investigator (2013). Tracing Quotations. Albert Einstein's quote. Retrieved October 29, 2024, from quoteinvestigator.com

Schultz, H. & Gordon, J. (2011) Onward: How Starbucks Fought for Its Life without Losing Its Soul. ISBN 978-1-60961-382-2

Toffler, A. (1984). Future Shock. ISBN-13 978-0808501527. Turtleback Books. In Forbes.com (2022, April 08).

Wilson Schaef, A. (n. d.). Brainy Quote. Retrieved October 19, 2024, from https://www.brainyquote.com/quotes/anne_wilson_schaef_169939

Unlocking Your Superconscious Potential

Superconscious Transformations

Walking the superconscious path

A few testimonials:

I met Anthony Williams in a time when I felt stuck and needed help. I suffered from physical issues that I felt was mostly coming out of my mental state. His approach and recode sessions [QRP] helped me immensely. He led our sessions with kindness and a firm structure. Because of that, I felt much more secure in myself and could open more to the process.

By the time I had my first session with Anthony I was really in pain (suffering from a frozen shoulder). Session after session my overall conditioning really improved not just mentally, but also my physical issue.

Unlocking Your Superconscious Potential

I am very thankful for all his help! It means very much to me! – Professional Photographer (Tina)

I have had astronomical growth since starting this program. It has helped me in numerous ways. My thinking process is now different, because I now understand I control my emotions, what I think, and therefore get to choose my life's experience. I just have to remember what I put out in the universe is coming back to me. So, I am now very mindful of what I say; and progressively becoming the predominant creative force in my life.

By allowing my Superconscious to be connected into, my confidence level has grown tremendously! I have learned not to hesitate nor be afraid to make decisions or stand up for myself. I [believe] in myself again, and standing behind my decisions; personally, and professionally.

- HR Professional (Monica Smith)

Gratitude. My confidence is through the roof! This program has helped me elevate to a higher level of understanding. I have less stress, and it provides me with exercises to continue my growth in all areas. I would definitely say go for it! - IT Professional (name omitted for privacy)

Q &A Session:

1. What were your initial goals when you entered the coaching program?

To achieve some tangible monetary goals related to a pending lawsuit and the opening of my consulting business.

2. How did you find out about the coaching program?
Via my network.

3. On a scale of 1 to 10, how would you rate your overall coaching experience? (1 being poor, 10 being excellent)
Overall a 10. I loved how you combined several modalities to consider the multifaceted nature of your clients. It felt like life-coaching merged with spiritual and cognitive coaching [and] development. It's clear that you really know your stuff! You broke things down for me to understand, and even used a whiteboard and other items to demonstrate your points. You were surprisingly

patient and empathetic. You were also reliable, showing up consistently for me and reminding me throughout the week to do the exercises and 'homework'.

4. What specific skills or insights did you gain from the coaching sessions?
Putting visualizations in a picture frame and placing them in the back of my mind. Properly managing my emotions because we can inadvertently manifest what we don't want while exerting strong negative emotions [and] thinking deeply about any given negative thing/situation.

5. Were there any challenges you faced during the coaching process? If so, how did your coach help you overcome them?
I'm a very literal and practical person, so sometimes, it could be difficult to visualize what has not yet manifested. Tony, you worked with me using different methods of getting past that, specifically helping me through taking my time to practice using my emotions [and] my mind's eye simultaneously.

6. Can you describe a breakthrough moment you had during coaching?

Yes, I've always thought of myself as a loner, with no support or cheerleaders in my corner, BUT the exercise where you had me picture a stadium full of my ancestors was the most impactful EVER! I still use that to help me raise my vibrations, at times. That was a game-changer for me!

7. How has coaching impacted on your personal and/or professional life?

Well, I was able to pay off my mortgage with the settlement that I received. I'm working on the business side of things now. I probably need more coaching.

8. Would you recommend this coaching program to others? Why or why not?
I definitely would, however, I'm sure the individual would have to be open minded, able to think outside the box, and a truth-seeker. Limiting beliefs and thinking have no place in this space.

Final Thoughts:

9. What did you appreciate most about your coach's style or approach?

I think I may have answered this in my above answers

10. Is there anything you would like to see improved in the coaching program?

It would have been nice to be able to refer back to some tangible resources and materials, other than my notes. Maybe create a booklet that has each session's topic outlined(?)

11. Any additional comments or insights you'd like to share?
No

Permission: **
12. May we use your testimonial for promotional purposes? (Yes/No)

Yes. Mrs. Erika Miller

Now listen when I tell you that none of the above has anything to do with me, Anthony Williams, it is the process at work. Let's look elsewhere. While I was being mentored in this work another mentee who was blind for more than 20 years regained his sight.

Countless others went on to start businesses when before the coaching they could not; they were stuck or oscillating, to include yours truly. Some became public speakers who before were afraid to talk in front of one person. Tap into your superconscious mind and become your own superhero. And Mrs. Erika Miller now you have a whole book, "Unlocking Your Superconscious Potential" at your disposal.

About the Author

Anthony L. Williams is a seasoned leader, a former Marine, and a dedicated advocate for personal transformation. After a distinguished career in the Marine Corps, where he inspired countless individuals to reach their full potential, Anthony embarked on a mission to help people worldwide unlock their true selves.

Driven by his own journey of overcoming adversity, Anthony developed a profound understanding of the human mind and its limitless potential. Anthony has dedicated his life to sharing these insights and empowering others to create extraordinary lives.

As a renowned transformational coach, Anthony guides individuals to tap into their superconscious mind, a realm of infinite possibilities. Through Anthony's work, he challenges limiting beliefs, empowers individuals to break free from self-imposed limitations, and inspires them to live with intention and purpose.

Anthony has stated in the past, "when we can change our mental state, we would have changed our future." In this work, Unlocking Your Superconscious

Potential, Anthony explains the mechanics of our minds and how to escape the box of conformity.

Anthony's unique approach blends ancient wisdom with modern science, providing practical tools and techniques to help individuals achieve lasting transformation. Anthony's passion for empowering others, coupled with his unwavering belief in the human spirit, has made him a sought-after mentor and a catalyst for positive change.

Anthony's commitment to empowering women is evident in his work. Anthony believes that by empowering women, we can create a more compassionate and harmonious world. Anthony's mission is to inspire women to rise to their full potential and lead with courage and compassion. Anthony believes we should empower women, since as he put it, one reason being, they are the ones raising our nation (children).

NOTES

NOTES

A Comprehensive Analysis of "Unlocking Your Superconscious Potential"

Introduction

The book "Unlocking Your Superconscious Potential" presents a compelling exploration of the human mind. The book delves into the depths of consciousness that offers practical tools for personal transformation. The author, Anthony L Williams, skillfully weaves together ancient wisdom, modern science, and personal anecdotes to create a comprehensive guide to unlocking the extraordinary potential within us.

Key Themes and Arguments

Williams' words revolves around the central premise that we are not merely passive observers of lives but active creators of our realities. Williams introduces the concept of the superconscious mind which is, a realm beyond human conscious awareness. The superconscious mind, holds the key to unlocking humans' true potentials.

Unlocking Your Superconscious Potential

Williams delves into the intricate relationship between the self-conscious, subconscious, and superconscious minds. This complex relationship explores the way in which limiting beliefs, societal expectations, and subconscious conditioning can hinder humans' progress and create a sense of stagnation. Williams emphasizes the importance of nnerstanding these factors and, then, taking steps to reprogram them.

Throughout Unlocking Your Superconscious Potential, Williams presents a wealth of practical tools and techniques for tapping into the superconscious mind. These tools include meditation, visualization, journaling, nature immersion, and the term Williams coined as the quantum reordering process (QRP). Williams provides clear instructions and guidance that make these practices accessible to all readers.

Evaluation of the Author's Expertise

Williams demonstrates a deep innerstanding of the subject matter by, drawing from a wide range of sources that encompass ancient wisdom, modern science, and personal experience. Williams' writing style is engaging and accessible; thus, making complex concepts easy to innerstand. Williams' passion on this subject is evident throughout his book. This passion can inspire readers to embark on their own journeys of self-discovery.

Strengths of the Book

- **Comprehensive Coverage:** Unlocking Your Superconscious Potential covers a wide range of topics related to the superconscious mind that transcends from ancient wisdom to modern science.

- **Practical Tools:** Williams provides clear and actionable steps for readers to apply the principles discussed in Unlocking Your Superconscious Potential.

- **Engaging Writing Style:** Unlocking Your Superconscious Potential is well-written and easy to follow, which makes it accessible to a broad audience.

- **Inspirational Message:** Williams' message of empowerment and personal transformation is inspiring and motivating.

Areas for Improvement

While Unlocking Your Superconscious Potential is generally well-structured and informative, there is room for further improvement:

- **Scientific Evidence:** Although Williams draws on scientific research to support some of his claims, Unlocking Your Superconscious Potential could benefit from more in-depth citations and references to scientific studies.

- **Case Studies:** Incorporating more case studies of individuals who have successfully applied the techniques in Unlocking Your Superconscious Potential could make the concepts more relatable and tangible.

- **Cultural Sensitivity:** Unlocking Your Superconscious Potential could benefit from a more diverse range of examples, as per qualitative studies and cross-sectional studies to ensure that the content is culturally sensitive and inclusive.

Overall Assessment

"Unlocking Your Superconscious Potential" is a valuable resource for anyone seeking to innerstand the depths of the human mind and harness its power for personal transformation. Williams' expertise, combined with the practical tools and insights he provided, make his book a valuable addition to the field of personal development.

Conclusion

In conclusion, "Unlocking Your Superconscious Potential" offers a comprehensive exploration of the human mind and its potential for transformation. By innerstanding the nature of the superconscious mind, the subconscious, and the self-conscious, readers can gain precious insights into their own lives and unlock their extraordinary potentials. Unlocking Your Superconscious Potential is a resourceful treasure trove for anyone seeking personal growth, empowerment, and a deeper innerstanding of themselves.

Note: While Unlocking Your Superconscious Potential provides a solid foundation for personal growth, it's important to note that the concept of the "superconscious mind" is not a universally accepted scientific term. It's a more metaphysical or spiritual concept that may not be fully supported by empirical evidence.

As an academic, it's crucial to approach such topics with a critical eye, that balances personal experiences and anecdotal evidences with rigorous scientific research. By integrating both scientific and spiritual perspectives, readers can gain a more comprehensive innerstanding of the human mind and its potential.

Dr. Ann-Marie Anthony-Williams
Applied Psychologist

Reading List

YOU'RE NOT BROKEN By Christopher M. Duncan

BECOMING SUPERNATURAL By Dr. Joe Dispenza

You Are the PLACEBO By Dr. Joe Dispenza

THE BIOLOGY OF BELIEF By Bruce H. Lipton, PH.D.

INSPIRATION CORNER By Anthony L. Williams

www.ingramcontent.com/pod-product-compliance
Lightning Source LLC
Chambersburg PA
CBHW032226080426
42735CB00008B/733